The
BEAUTY
THERAPIST'S
Handbook

Joy Morris
FSB Th, BABTAC, FEd TCert

B T Batsford Limited, London

© Joy Morris 1987
First published 1987

All rights reserved. No part of this publication
may be reproduced, in any form or by any means,
without permission from the Publisher

Typeset by Servis Filmsetting Ltd, Manchester
and printed in Great Britain by
The Bath Press
Bath
for the publishers
B T Batsford Limited
4 Fitzhardinge Street
London W1H 0AH

British Library Cataloguing in Publication Data

Morris, Joy
  The beauty therapists handbook.—
  (Vocational studies).—(A Batsford book).
  1. Beauty, Personal
  I. Title ·II. Series
  646.7′2′088042   RA778

ISBN 0-7134-5295-1

Contents

and film make-up artists. Electrolysis clinics. Technical representatives. Beauty on wheels. Teaching Beauty Therapy. The beauty journalist. Beauty therapy abroad. Working in the EEC. Beauty in the Middle East. Beauty the American way. Beauty Down Under. Beauty in the Far East. Beauty in South Africa. Beauty around the world

4 Treatment planning   69

Treatment planning. Body treatments: Posture; Weight; Client co-operation; Dietary advice; Movement and exercise; Treatments available. Assessing the less overweight. Contra-indications. Body massage. Reflexology. Running the figure clinic. Safety in the sun-bed room: Shower facilities. Keeping records. The face clinic. Facial analysis. Diagnosing skin types. Planning a treatment programme. Laser therapy. Electrolysis. Ancillary treatments. Promoting treatments. Retail selling: Dealing with complaints; Safety in the salon

5 A salon of your own   106

A working plan. Financing the plan. Overdraft or loan? Buying an existing business. Buying a salon with freehold property. Buying a business in a leasehold premises. Starting from scratch. What type of premises? Sharing premises. Renting a chair. Parking facilities. Back to a plan again: salon layout. Equipment to buy or to lease? New or secondhand? Hire purchase or leasing? Keeping things ticking. Protection by insurance

6 Salon success   129

The treatment brochure. Old faithfuls: classic treatments. Price list or brochure? Printing your masterpiece. Naming the salon. Advertising and public relations. Show a pretty face. Beginners' blues. New ideas. First employee. Choosing the right person

Acknowledgment

I would like to offer my sincere thanks to all the people who willingly answered my many questions and particularly those individuals and companies who so kindly loaned me photographs for illustrations, especially Mrs I Graham of Depilex; Mr R Fabes of Taylor Reeson Ltd; Mr M Shirley of Clarins (UK), Mrs Dorothy Parkes of The British Association of Beauty Therapy and Cosmetology and Mrs June Simmonds of The International Health and Beauty Council.

My sincere thanks also go to all my international colleagues, too numerous to mention individually, who so readily sent me information regarding beauty therapy in their countries. My grateful thanks also to Norman Morris for his technical work on the manuscript and to Thelma Nye, Technical editor of Batsfords for her patience and kindness.

Bristol 1987   JM

Introduction to beauty

Beauty as it was

Since the dawn of time and man's awareness of his own body, both the male and the female of the species have sought to alter and improve their appearance.

Early civilisations, primitive as they were, observed nature and the wonders of natural camouflage. They marvelled at the degree of protection that some of the other animals achieved through their natural colouring and formation which sometimes rendered them indistinguishable from their environment. Being the thinking species, man soon realised that he could imitate nature by camouflaging himself and acquire a certain amount of protection from other tribes and marauding animals.

Painting as camouflage

So was born the art of painting the face and body. It did not take long for man to realise that he could also use this form of painting to appear far more frightening, and thus began a ritual of painting horrific patterns to intimidate and frighten the enemy; a ritual which is still to be found in the primitive tribes in the jungles of South America and the aboriginal tribes of Australia.

As this paint was applied just before going into battle, and the help of the gods was being called upon, the two became intertwined and the whole process became part of a ritualistic symbolism. It may be that primitive woman preferred the male with the most interesting and fearsome painting, for it soon became part of the courtship act for the male and female to paint themselves in order to attract the opposite sex.

Materials used

A far cry from the modern beauty world one might think, but not so far removed when you think of the materials used.

Primitive man did not have years of cosmetic chemistry expertise behind him. All he had were the natural things that grew around him. Plants, flowers, vegetables, natural earths, and fats from the animals he had killed. These he skilfully learned to blend together to form his paints. In the gathering and use of the natural things, not only for paint but for food as well, man soon realised that some plants had either good or bad effects on the human body. Cuts and injuries received when hunting could be cured by applying the leaves or juices of certain plants; sickness from eating unfit food could be eased by consuming yet another plant. So we see, right from the beginning of time, the art of treating and healing the body had been developing along with man's knowledge of himself and his environment. As each successive civilisation came and went, it developed still further the art of treating the body, inside and out, in sickness and in health.

Many cosmetic art forms originated through a need to protect the body. For instance, daubing the skin with a mixture of clay mud and animal fats not only frightened the enemy but also helped protect the skin from scratches and cuts while out hunting, and shielded the skin from the strong rays of the sun. Eyeliner, so beloved by ancient Egyptians, originated from the need in hot countries to surround the eye with certain herbal ointments to discourage the flies from settling around the eyes as they do on animals, and thus preventing eye diseases.

Early Chinese dynasties

Each successive generation learned the secrets and cures of their fathers, and went on to evolve more as their knowledge of themselves, and the world about them, grew. As travelling became more widespread, so such knowledge was passed on to other nations. Each group of people developed their own particular methods and ideas for which they became famed. The early Chinese perfected the techniques of **homeopathy**, which is a method of curing by using concentrated doses of pure herbs and plant derivatives. They also evolved, right at the beginning of their cultural development, a method of curing ills, and also preventing illness, by means of sticking sharp needles into the skin and rotating them very quickly. **Acupuncture**, as this technique is now called, appears to be as old as the Chinese race itself. It fell into disrepute in the western world for years when it seemed that if a method could not be explained precisely, then it was disregarded as being of no account. Thank goodness a more enlightened attitude exists today, and many people are seeking and getting relief from many western ailments by the use of the acupuncturists' needles.

Egyptian culture

Whilst the Chinese were busy perfecting their skills, the Egyptians on the other side of the world were developing into one of the most knowledgeable and sophisticated cultures. Their knowledge of herbs and perfumes was extensive. Containers and dishes found in the pyramids, and now in museums all over the world, show that they were practised in the art of making all different kinds of ointments and creams, and loved anointing their bodies with oils and lotions. Possibly because of the heat of their country, they were obsessed with personal cleanliness and started the practice of removing all body and facial hair. The wealthier Egyptians shaved their heads, and had the now familiar looking dark wigs and ornately jewelled headdresses made to wear when they left the confines of their homes.

Baths as we know them did not appear until the Greco/Roman period, but the early Egyptians certainly had shower rooms. Excavation of early villas show conclusively that all wealthy Egyptians not only had shower rooms, but also massage and oil anointing rooms alongside them. Uncovered in the early excavations of the great pyramid tomb of Tutankhamen was an unguent jar still containing a cosmetic made from animal fats, herbs, spices and perfumes.

The great queen Cleopatra inherited all the knowledge and wealth of this famous civilisation, and has remained a firm favourite throughout the ages as she personifies all that was Egypt.

Like all the members of her race, both male and female, she loved colour – the more vibrant the better. Their naturally dark skins showed off the jewel-bright colours that they wore to perfection. However, it was thought that the female Egyptian should have lighter skin tones than the male. There is recorded evidence that the women attempted to bleach their skins slightly in order to achieve a lighter skin tone, but it appears that Cleopatra did not need such treatment as she was naturally lighter toned. They perfected the art of cosmetic adornment of the face, and used their love of vibrant colours to enhance their eyes with elaborate make-up.

The most distinctive part of their eye make-up was the very liberal use of the black eyeliner called *kohl*. This was usually made of antimony or lead sulphide, and incorporated into it was the special ointment intended to ward off flies and subsequent infections of the eyes.

The first book on beauty

The Egyptian sophistication did not end at the eye make-up. The women stained their cheeks with a rouge made from red ochre and an animal fat, their hands and feet were tinted with henna and there is evidence to show that they painted the rest of their bodies as well. The interesting thing about the Egyptian culture was the development of skin care treatments. Cleopatra is reputed to have written a book on caring for the skin, and excavations of the tombs in latter years have produced a whole range of artifacts used in the pursuit of this. The tombs yielded a treasure trove of small implements such as strygils (small bone spatulas used for scraping away the top layers of dead cells on the skin), early forms of razors, pumice stones, eyebrow tweezers and countless jars of creams, oils, and ointments. These all give support to the theory that cosmetically the Egyptians were the most advanced culture around at that time.

Other Mediterranean cultures

As with other civilisations, the travelling Egyptians took with them their arts and crafts, which were adopted by other races around the Mediterranean. The Assyrians and Babylonians adopted the Egyptian mode of lining their eyes, but the rest of their make-up was not so exotic.

The Assyrian fighting men adopted this method of making up as part of their battle dress to scare the enemy. It seems that the wheel went full circle, from early primitive man using his camouflage to intimidate his enemy.

Other civilisations around the middle east had also adopted the fashion of facial cosmetics. There are plenty of references in the Bible to the fact that Hebrew women were now copying their Egyptian sisters, although the use of facial cosmetics was frowned upon in many instances. Perhaps the most famous instance was Jezabel, who was renowned for her very elaborate forms of facial make-up. However, it is interesting to note that unlike the Egyptians, Hebrew men never wore make-up.

Grecian beauty

Greek males did not wear make-up either. Much lighter in skin tone colours, the Greeks were a race that preferred a much more subtle and delicate approach than the early Egyptians. The Greek culture loved elegance and moderation in all things. Greek men were renowned for their athletic prowess, and developed great exercise and play routines to keep their bodies fit and well. The only cosmetic used by Greek men appeared to be hair dyes. The women used very little face paint but many creams were formulated and used in an attempt to lighten the skin, as a lighter skin was held to be more feminine. So their cosmetics seem to have been confined to skin care and hair care range rather than painting the face. The Greek woman was dominated by her male counterpart, and it became the accepted thing that 'respectable' women did not use facial cosmetics. This was left to the courtesan who painted her face liberally to advertise her calling!

As with all these middle eastern races, bathing and personal hygiene played a great part in the daily lives of the Greek household. They added to the worlds knowledge of the use of oils and aromatic herbs to produce perfumes, much of this knowledge being copied and absorbed by yet another great civilisation who perfected it even further – the Romans.

Rome and its Baths

Like the other races mentioned, the Romans were devoted to their personal hygiene and also loved bathing. The famous Roman baths, which were erected as part of every Roman villa, also contained small side rooms, as had the early Egyptian dwellings. These side rooms were for personal ablutions, such as removing completely all body and facial hair. Roman men, however, did not shave their heads like the Egyptians but they kept their hair short with their distinctive bob, and made sure they were clean shaven everywhere else.

Roman citizens not wealthy enough to have their own baths incorporated into their homes, would frequent the public baths and depilatory shops where they could be bathed and shaved by slaves. The Romans were also fond of anointing the body with oils, mainly in the belief that such oils and lotions kept away infections. Combined with the strict personal hygiene of the race, it probably did.

Roman women, however, were much more liberated than their Greek sisters and used facial cosmetics liberally. A fine creamy skin, free from blemishes, was considered to be the height of good breeding and fine fashion. Cold cream is reputed to have been invented by Galen, a physician in Rome, and with only slight modifications, his recipe is still the basis of our present cold cream formula.

With the coming of the northern slaves from Britain and

Germany with their pale skins, the Roman women began to use bleach and white based cosmetics in an attempt to appear to have a lighter skin tone. They also tried bleaching their hair blonde. Possibly again to imitate the pale and classical looks of the northern slaves which seemed to excite the Roman male so much. However, they do not appear to have been too successful with their bleaches, as it has been recorded that they constantly wore wigs, made from the hair of the captured Gaulish women to cover up their own poor growths of hair.

Their constant quest for a perfect pale skin also began to take its toll as the cosmetics they used were usually a white lead derivative. This had a very poisonous and destructive effect on the skin and sent the ladies scurrying to every seller of ointments and creams in search of an antidote to restore them, at least, to their former looks.

The Roman lady of fashion appears to be the first to have openly attended a beauty salon. Special rooms were set aside at the popular baths for the painting of the face after the lady had bathed and had her body massaged with oils. These establishments then became questionable as the young males about town began hanging around them in attempts to seduce the more attractive, wealthy, or influential women.

Anglo-Saxon Britain

Britain at this time was still in a very wild, uncivilised state. Sharply divided into tribal areas, it had little or no culture other than the religious cult of the early Druids. The tribes were, of course, still in the stage of wearing war paint to frighten and intimidate their enemies. In fact the Picts were so called because the name meant 'The painted ones'. However, the Druidic culture fostered and encouraged the eternal quest for curative creams and medicines among the natural herbs and plantlife. In later years this natural folklore, which was handed down from generation to generation, caused many medieval exponents to be branded witch or warlock because they had such uncanny skills in curing every conceivable ill through the use of plants and herbs.

Although early British women did not have cosmetics they had the one thing that the Romans desired most – heads of glorious thick long golden hair! This they wore either loose and unbraided if they were unmarried, or plaited and braided if they were. Their men also grew their hair very long and seemed to outdo the women on occasions.

Through a series of invasions the Anglo Saxons continued in the same manner until the Norman Conquest. The Normans brought many of the sophisticated and softer customs of France with them, and these gradually became assimilated into the British way of life. Facial cosmetics was not one of them; these were not to make an appearance in Britain until the end of the Crusades. Men who had travelled the East and all around the Mediterranean civilisations had become accustomed to the exotic perfumes and colours of the east. Eastern women, much darker skinned than the wives they left at home, must have looked very alluring with their soft dark skin and their lovely dark eyes accentuated by kohl and other eye make-up. Queen Eleanor, wife of England's Henry II, went on a crusade herself with an army of women. It is said that she brought back to England and France many of the cosmetic arts she had seen abroad. Whatever pressures were put upon them, the British women appear to have resisted any attempt to darken their skins at that time.

Early medieval faces

In Britain, as in France and Italy, the fashion then became the pale flat, perfect oval face that we see looking out at us from medieval paintings. Hair was strained back under elaborate headdresses and the face was made to look even more uninteresting by the removal of all the eyebrows and hairline. It seems that whatever the French women did, the British copied, albeit sometimes in a more subdued and modified manner.

Cosmetics were being imported from France by the more daring, but on the whole it was not the thing to do as the Church was against it, and at that time the Church had a great hold over the ordinary people. So for many years, whilst dress fashions altered, the desire to keep their complexions as pale and free from freckles as possible seemed to be all that interested British women. In the search for this, they went to great lengths to obtain recipes for creams claimed to whiten the skin. Possibly due to the extremely poor hygiene and stuffy homes, records show they spent a great deal of their time and energy preparing floral pomanders, room fresheners, toilet waters and other aromatic perfumes to take away the smells and to ward off germs. Italian women by this time were certainly painting their faces.

The First Elizabethan Age

At the time Elizabeth I came to the throne, fashions were brought to the English court by the Italian and French ambassadors and their entourages. The cosmetic fashions they had brought with them were still very similar to the Roman idea – a white powdered face, rouged cheeks and red or carmine lip colouring. With the Queen having naturally light red hair, it also became the fashion to dye the hair in an attempt to achieve similar colouring. After dyeing her hair, whitening her face with the deadly and poisonous white lead powder, applying red ochre rouge, the fashionable woman would then paint it all over with the clear varnish glaze of the white of an egg. Recipes would change hands from lady to lady each with her own personal beauty secrets, mostly of creams reputed to be marvellous for whitening the skin of the face and hands. If all else failed, they could always resort to the masks that were fast becoming the fashion for both men and women.

Although very dandified in their elaborate manner of dress, the Elizabethan men did not use cosmetics. They wore the usual heavy perfumes of the age and dyed their hair, but there is no record of facial cosmetics being favoured by any of them.

James and his painted man

This is more than can be said for the early Jacobean court. Because of the King's preference for men, the fashion of heavily painted male faces became very much the 'in thing'. The ladies too had by this time a large selection of foreign and homemade cosmetics from which to choose, mainly purchased from the tinker or pack men who travelled the country. London ladies had the pleasure of buying theirs along with their ribbons, gloves and hats at the more fashionable shops in St James's.

The work of the Devil!

The growing tide of Puritanism was soon to raise its voice against the art of painting and powdering, railed at by Church leaders as being the work of the devil. The execution of Charles I, and the Cromwellian government being in power meant the end of any such practices. It was said that one lady of the manor was denounced as a witch by one of her servants because she innocently gathered herbs and oils to make herself some hand cream!

With the restoration of the monarchy, there came back all the old cosmetic arts and many more. Ladies took to wearing artificial eyebrows, wigs or hairpieces and many were receiving attention from the growing band of surgeons dealing with the teeth. Elaborate dressing-table sets were the craze to hold all the various false bits and pieces of a lady of fashion.

Despite the sophisticated make-up it was difficult to hide the ravages of the face caused by the many diseases which prevailed at that time. The most damaging of which was smallpox. This left the face with very badly disfiguring scars and pockmarks. The fashion of wearing patches on the face, usually of black velvet or a fabric to match the wearer's outfit, came into being to disguise these marks. The rages of the white lead-based cosmetics were also telling on some skins, and one famous beauty of the time retired to die in her country home, hidden from the world, her face badly eaten into, and her whole system poisoned by lead.

French influence

In France at this time small salons were being set up by quack medical men and hairdressers, where men and ladies of fashion could get their hair and wigs dressed, receive massage and depilation and any other cosmetic treatment they needed. Once again though, as in the salons of Roman times, the salons earned a bad reputation as being brothels or places where assignations were made. In London the small shops in St James's were frequented by the fashionable in their eternal quest for new and exciting cosmetics. Many such shops had a small treatment room at the rear, but it was certainly not the fashion to admit to having received any treatment there.

Regency style

As with all fashions there comes a swing in the opposite direction. During the mid-eighteenth century people began to shun the overpainted face, and the general preference was for the more natural look. By the end of the century the use of all cosmetics was frowned upon and the regency lady was deeply involved with the growing fashion in Britain of washing and bathing regularly instead of painting over the dirt. The soap industry was well and truly under way with many famous soap firms, in existence to this day, beginning to make their appearance. Women's magazines were appearing with articles on making some skin care products. British water must have played havoc with their hands because so many of the recipes were for creams to soften and whiten the hands. The use of a very modest and delicate amount of rouge was permitted, but it was expected to be discreet. Anything that looked at all painted immediately brought the label 'brazen, immodest, vulgar'.

Victorian attitudes

This attitude increased with the coronation of the young but prudish Queen Victoria. 'Respectable' ladies did not dare to flout convention. The few beauty salons that did exist were small discreet places, without any form of advertisement. Carriages with heavily curtained windows would wait at the rear of such premises for Madam to slip, unrecognised, out of a rear exit. The reputation of these salons was not enhanced by an infamous court case in which the proprietress was prosecuted for blackmailing a client. Slowly times were changing though and famous socialites and actresses were allowing their names and faces to be used as advertisements firstly for soaps, then for face creams. Steadily and surely the pedulum of fashion was beginning to swing again.

Emancipation of women

Two world wars, the emancipation of women, and a drastic rise in the standard of living for the ordinary people, completely revolutionised the world of beauty.

The emancipated woman, freed from the strict confines of social etiquette of bygone days, and with the opportunity of earning and spending her own money, did exactly as she wished. If visiting a beauty salon was one of those wishes, then nobody stopped her, and beauty salons opened with surprising alacrity to cater for the new modern miss.

Between the wars, beauty became big business mainly in London, although some of the larger cities in the provinces had their share of salons. To begin with they were mainly hairdressing salons with a few discreet rooms curtained off for the provision of hair removal and manicures. However, since the Second World War and the rise in the technical standards of beauty therapy training, reliable beauty salons are to be found throughout the world. These provide beauty treatments of the highest standard and most are in the financial reach of the majority of women.

In latter years the wheel has turned full circle and the fashion is once again to use the natural plant and herbal creams and aromatic oils of our primitive forefathers. Ancient treatments such as acupuncture and acupressure are helping to reduce the strain of modern living, proving once more that nothing under the sun is new; it is either in or out of fashion.

Since the emancipation of women the fashion has not been so much whether or not to wear make-up but how to wear it.

Each successive generation of women seem to develop their own style of make-up, and these are fascinating to recall. The full bloomed, heavy bosomed look of the Edwardian beauties gave way to the pale, little-girl-lost look of the early cinema heroines played so beautifully on the silent screen by Mary Pickford. Quite a contrast in styles. Again an enormous contrast when Theda Barry stormed on to the silver screen with her vamp look. Heavily ringed eye make-up and glossy cupid bow lips were her hall-mark, and every factory girl and shop assistant who could afford the price of a cinema ticket became sultry sirens the next day. Make-up was being mass produced and was well within their pockets.

Regrettably the quality of that make-up left much to be desired and dermatology clinics were being set up all over the country in an attempt to counteract the skin problems brought about by the use of cheap cosmetics.

The talkies came, and with them a small army of screen favourites for the ordinary girls to copy. The cool icy classical beauty of Greta Garbo, the thinly plucked eyebrows that were the hallmark of Marlene Dietrich, the blonde hair of Jean Harlow and many others, set up minor fashions of their own. Vivien Leigh, Margaret Lockwood, Jean Kent and Diana Dors, all created make-up fashions for the girl in the street to imitate. Then came television and a whole host of other faces that became famous bringing with them a distinctive style all of their own. In recent years, however, the fashion tends to be more individual with every woman doing her own thing, wearing the make-up fashion or style or colouring which suits her best. This adds more individuality to the scene and creates a great deal of interest in the kind of services that the beauty salon can offer. Women are also much more aware that cosmetic fashions can come and go, but if they do not have a good skin on which to apply them, the desired look is not achieved.

1 The client/therapist relationship

Beauty therapy, an art or a science?

The world of beauty is changing and maturing. Gone fortunately, are the days of the old images of luxurious and very expensive salons, worked by ill trained but glamorous staff. Slowly but surely the general public are beginning to realise that Beauty Therapy and all it entails is a very skilled occupation which requires a formal, technical and scientific training as well as a great deal of artistic interpretion. Thanks to modern technology, the beauty salon can now offer sane and sensible treatments at prices the average woman in the street can afford. Despite the economic situation, and the forecasts of scarcity of money for luxury items, the world of beauty is one of the fastest growing areas of the leisure industry. As in any other profession there are areas where work is scarce, but if the therapist is as fully qualified as she can be and is prepared to move around in search of work, then there are great potentials in this very satisfying and rewarding career.

What makes a good therapist?

Let us look then at the beauty therapist herself? What kind of person and temperament is best suited to this work? It is fairly obvious that the girl who enters beauty therapy thinking that it is a light superficial job, looking glamorous and doing little else is in for a big shock! Anyone who wishes to become a good therapist must have a quiet, sympathetic caring quality which is so essential in order to building up that all important client/therapist rapport. It is important to acquire the ability to put everyone at their ease and also to be a good listener. The therapist has to be capable of listening to a wide range of problems not only of a beauty nature but also on many personal subjects such as the client's work, her family, or her personal relationships. The client often feels the need to confide in someone. Quite naturally the therapist must respect these confidences and keep them strictly to herself. She must remain even tempered and calm at all times in order to gain the client's confidence and to relax her. The client may appear calm and in control, but often this will not be the true case.

Looking the part

The beauty therapist does not need to be a born beauty, but she must exercise all her skills and training on herself first and appear as glamorous and well groomed as possible in order to impress her clients. No one would really feel that they could accept the advice of someone who did not practise what they preached.

She must also be a very fit and healthy person who is able to withstand a very physically tiring day. The beauty salon works extremely long hours so the therapist must also be at the peak of mental as well as physical fitness and absolutely exuding health and vitality. After all, these are the aims and objectives strived at for the client so why not the same for the therapist?

The therapist must also be within a few pounds of her target weight. It is all very well to have a weight problem, and when dealing with the overweight client it can be a positive advantage; however it must be a weight problem which is strictly under control. The therapist can help the client by sympathising with her, but she can also demonstrate in a positive way that the problem can be controlled.

Whatever exercise routine the therapist recommends for her client, she must, quite naturally, be able to perform herself so that she can demonstrate it effectively, always bearing in mind that when one recommends either a dietary or vigorous exercise routine, the client should be advised to consult her GP for permission before embarking on a change in her lifestyle.

Young or mature?

The person training to be a beauty therapist need not necessarily be a young girl. It is an ideal profession for the mature woman looking for a second career, and although the training is intensive it is not beyond the capabilities of most women who seriously want to do the work and are therefore interested in learning. A properly trained beauty teacher is skilled in coping with students of differing age groups and the younger students tend to appreciate having an older woman in the group.

Building a rapport with the clients

Whether young or mature the successful beauty therapist is the one who shows that she really cares about her clients and can change to suit the individual needs of each and every one however different they may be. Although she must be a good listener, there are times when it is necessary to be a reassuring 'ego booster'. Not only should she be fully trained but also she must be prepared to keep learning in her quest to help the clients who consult her.

The beauty salon itself should be a very special place for the clients. Of course, it needs to be glamorous and elegant, because that is part of the dream wish for which the client is paying, but it must also be a haven of rest and relaxation. It must be a place where she can immediately feel at ease and relax without feeling uncomfortable or intimidated. Somewhere where she knows she will always find someone who will listen. A place where she can shut herself away from the outside world and just be herself, if only for a few hours at a time. In this stress orientated world of today the most successful salons are those that care for their clients with a capital 'C' and, bearing all these points in mind, satisfy their clients' every need.

Who are the clients and why do they seek treatment?

So who are the clients and why do they come to the salon in the first place? Most would reply 'for the treatment, of course', but is this really so? Firstly let us ask ourselves who the clients really are? Leaving aside a few exclusive salons that could show you a clientele list of famous people to rival the latest edition of *Who's Who*, the average client of today's beauty salon is a very ordinary lady. In the early sixties one could safely say that the clients came from a very narrow section of the class structure within a rigid age and financial status range. Not however in the eighties!

The ages of clients attending any salon or health and beauty establishment today could be anything between the ages of sixteen and eighty! The younger client sees a visit to the salon or beauty room at the health club as a very common place and regular thing to do in order to have her legs waxed or her eyelashes tinted. The more mature ladies are also realising that the beauty salon is definitely the place to get help with the many problems that occur with ageing. So, as the age range of the client has widened considerably, has the class of the client also changed? The answer is a resounding yes!

While the clients of the sixties and earlier were only of the upper and upper middle class section of society, the clients of the eighties are most definitely classless! Experts studying the breakdown of the social class structure have put forward a variety of theories for the change in social attitudes, but they all acknowledge that nowhere is it more apparent than in the world of women. Changing attitudes towards the acceptance of women as equals and more specifically to women being paid as equals has helped considerably in breaking down class barriers in many ways.

Beauty breaks down barriers

It is the opinion of many sociologists that women of all classes, once freed from the rigid class structure of the home environment, found it easier to break through the class barriers than their male counterparts. Armed with a realistic wage that she had earned herself, the lower middle class and working class woman did not hesitate to avail themselves of the benefits of visiting the beauty salon. That it had traditionally been the province of the wealthy and famous mattered not one jot. If she could afford the treatment then she would have it!

This way of thinking greatly contributed to the boom in the cosmetic and beauty industries in the seventies. However, this attitude then raises the question, is the client really wanting the physical benefits of the treatment or the psychological reassurance that she is equal to any other woman? It could therefore be logically stated that the desire for social equality is one of the reasons why a woman seeks treatment. Having reassured herself that she has achieved social equality she then has to attempt the almost impossible task of moulding herself into the right 'image'. Despite the so often repeated message that now is the time for doing your own thing and being oneself, the media are still presenting an image which is subtlety portrayed as being the only successful type of woman.

The psychology of success

Certain physical attributes are shown as being acceptable, while others are not. A slim, youthful appearance, wearing this season's fashions is definitely 'right' while overweight, with superfluous hair and showing signs of ageing presents a definitely 'wrong' image. Hence the boom in the group therapy clubs and the huge growth in the multi-million pound 'slimming industry'. Leaving aside the medical campaign that encourages a few people to loose weight, it has been proven that the majority of women attend slimming clubs for appearance reasons more than for anything else.

Of all the mass media, television is the most guilty of 'image' making. A woman watching television sees a situation where the female character portrayed loosely fits her own way of life, she then feels that she must conform to that image.

Not only the casting directors of films and plays, but advertisers as well, find it necessary to stereotype the female character. If the advertisement is featuring a young married woman, then she must be portrayed as slim and attractive with hair that looks as if she has just left the hairdressers. Her make-up will be immaculate and her clothes will be fashionable, but not showy, even if she is only enthusing about the whiteness of her washing or the state of the kitchen floor she is supposed to have just washed!

Only if it is part of the plot will they deviate from this stereotype, and then they portray the 'failure' type as being possibly overweight, hair all over the place and looking at least as though she has done something. Older women are even more rigidly stereotypes, often with actresses some ten or fifteen years younger playing the parts of the more mature, middle aged woman. They must look as though they are growing old gracefully, certainly no mention of loosing their figures, teeth or hair. Even when a grandmother is portrayed there is seldom any individuality about it. In this instance white hair is a must, no shades of going grey, with a chubby angelic face and a serene countenance. Old age, vitriolic temperaments and rheumatism do not exist as far as television is concerned. Apart from the annual 'Glamorous Granny' competition, grannies do not wear high heels, high fashion or make-up.

Likewise, successful secretaries, PAs, or office girls are never overweight or spotty or suffering from premenstrual tension. Young mums are never scruffy with naughty children, and middle aged mums do not have hair on their faces. The inference being, that if they do, or are anything less than the image presented, then they are failures, not only to themselves but also to their families and loved ones.

It is little wonder then that women now feel the need to seek treatment in order to conform to these powerful images. Even our lady Prime Minister was urged to accept changes in her early years of office, in order that she should present a 'better' media image.

So, along with social equality, we can list social conformity and acceptability in the psychological need for treatment.

Why do they wish to look their best?

Leaving aside the external social pressures, we then come to the reasons that arise from within the client herself. These are the basic needs of all women regardless of culture, race or creed, and these needs are to be loved, to be attractive and admired, and to lead a happy and fulfilled life. These reasons often motivate a client to seek treatment, sometimes to please herself and sometimes to please a loved one.

Often a client will come on the pretext of receiving one kind of treatment, maybe a manicure, when they really need something more serious such as electrolysis. Admitting that they need help for what they consider to be a sign of failure on their part often takes a great deal of courage and many will attend the salon for some time before plucking up such courage to mention it.

Many come, regardless of the treatment they choose, just to receive cossetting and pampering from someone else. When ones' whole life revolves around taking care of a family and seeing to their every need, there is usually precious little time left to devote to oneself. This type of client revels in the few hours she has managed to put aside for herself in the beauty salon where she can be the sole beneficiary of all the pampering!

Sympathetic listening

Then there is the client that comes to talk! And how they talk! Very slowly at first, and on a superficial level with amusing little derogatory remarks about themselves until they are sure of the response they will receive from the Therapist. If reassured that she has a sympathetic listener, then quite subconsciously she will get down to the serious business; that of airing her deep down problems to someone who will listen without interruption. More importantly, that someone must be entirely independent and in no way connected or even remotely know the other characters involved in her personal problems. This is where the beauty therapist fits the bill. Just simply talking through the problem and putting into words her unspoken fears, bringing into the light parts of her problem that she had never faced before, often helps a client to work quietly out a solution to it.

The value of a good training

Obviously good beauty therapists are not born but made that way, and this is where the quality of a good beauty therapy training comes in. A college that conforms to the requirements of the three main examining bodies should offer that quality of training, by teaching not only the manual skills of the work but the professionalism as well.

When working in a community, constantly in touch with members of the general public, the reputation of the salon relies very heavily on the professionalism of the therapists that work there. A good reputation for giving value for money and for other things such as cleanliness, honesty and professional attitudes take a long time to build up, but regrettably can be destroyed extremely quickly. Professional attitudes are very difficult to define but also very noticeable when they are not there.

Professional organisations

In the early days of the profession there were several organisations set up with the intention of assisting people who were working in the world of beauty to get together and exchange ideas and views about the work, and to promote beauty therapy as a proper career. After a series of amalgamations we are left today with two main professional organisations of which the greatest proportion of working beauty therapists are members. They are **The International Federation of Health and Beauty Therapists**, and **The British Association of Beauty Therapy and Cosmetology**. Both of these institutions have their own examining boards and, along with the **City and Guilds of London Institute**, these examining boards are the ones with which most good colleges work. Both of the organisations mentioned have a set of rules by which their members agree to work and live. As with all professions, these sets of rules are called a *Code of Ethics*. These Codes have several purposes:

1 To protect the general public from improper practices being carried out in the name of Beauty Therapy.

2 To give guidance to the beauty therapist on what are acceptable standards and what are not.

3 To promote good relationships between beauty therapists not only within their own particular organisation but also within other organisations which uphold a good standard of training and subscribe to a similar Code of Ethics.

4 To establish a professional relationship between the profession of beauty therapists and other suitably qualified professions who have the care and welfare of the general public in their hands.

For the information of the student who has not yet obtained her professional status the following is an amalgamation of the Codes of Ethics of the two professional organisations of which I am a member. It is necessary to abide very strictly by these codes in order to work amicably in a community and gain the respect of other professional people.

Code of Ethics

1 All members of the organisation must agree to conform to the Code of Ethics, membership will not be granted without this specific agreement.

2 All members must at all times uphold the dignity of the profession and will conduct themselves in a professional manner at all times.

3 A member will not knowingly treat any person for a condition, who is at that time under the care of a registered medical practitioner without the express permission and consent of that medical practitioner. It is the duty of members to ascertain such information from the clients before the commencement of treatment.

4 No member shall give a treatment or prescribe any medicament or give any injections which should be prescribed by a medical practitioner.

5 A member must agree to respect the confidences of a client and never discuss a client or her problems with anyone else.

6 All members must respect the work of a fellow beauty therapist and must not criticise or comment on her work. At no time should a member attempt to encourage a client to leave a colleague and attend her establishment for treatment.

7 No member will ever perform a treatment knowing that the client has a condition which is listed as a contra-indication to that treatment.

8 All members will wear suitable professional clothing and will not work in an establishment where provocative clothing is worn or dubious treatments are performed or offered.

9 No member on leaving employment shall attempt to entice the clients of her former employer to become her clients or attend another establishment for treatment.

On reading this Code of Ethics one can see that it is a reasonable guide to a straight forward and honest way of working. By strictly adhering to it the beauty therapist can help establish both herself as a respected professional person and also beauty therapy as an ethical, caring profession.

2 The making of a good therapist

Training for beauty

As all the subjects covered under the general heading of health and beauty require a technical and detailed training, the choice of training establishment must be considered with great care.

It is impossible to learn on an apprenticeship or in a situation where a student is trained on the job. Anyone offering this kind of training would basically only be teaching a few practical skills, making the student really only employable by that establishment. No other employer in the field of health and beauty would consider accepting a therapist who had not completed an authentic course of training at an approved college, and had the necessary certificates to prove it.

An employer would be looking for proof that the applicant for a post had followed a recognised course of training and shown enough practical skill and theoretical knowledge to enable her to be awarded the necessary qualification diplomas and certificates.

In health and beauty therapy, as in other professions, there are many training courses and examination bodies that have been set up over the years, some good and some not so good. Without going into the politics of the situation, one can safely say that there are three main organisations offering syllabuses and examinations with which the majority of good colleges, both technical and private, comply. They are:

1 The City and Guilds of London Institute.

2 The Confederation of International Beauty Therapy and Cosmetology which is the educational and examination branch

of the British Association of Beauty Therapy and Cosmetology.

3 The International Health and Beauty Council which is the educational and examination branch of The International Federation of Health and Beauty Therapists. (This organisation also has within its jurisdiction an educational and examination branch called the International Institute of Sports Therapy.)

Although these three organisations have slightly different views on some aspects of the work, their basic approach to the teaching of the subject is the same, and their syllabuses in general cover the same amount of work and to the same depth of study.

Most good colleges offer a course of training covering the syllabuses and leading to both theoretical and practical examinations of one or often two of the above examination boards.

Which college?

It is apparent then that a great deal of thought should be given to the college you choose. Much will depend on your circumstances. The first choice will be between local education authority colleges of further and higher education (for simplicity these are referred to as technical colleges) and privately owned colleges.

The difference between these two types of colleges has on occasions been described as 'at private colleges you pay and at technical colleges you don't'. This of course is nonsense. The local education authority college makes a charge the same as the private ones, but if you manage to get a place in the local education authority college, it usually means you are eligible for a local education authority grant which pays all of or most of your fees. This in actual fact varies from one local education authority to another so no hard and fast rules can be applied. However, we can generalise and say that if you are a young person embarking on your first career training and have the necessary educational qualifications and have been accepted by the local technical college for training, then you stand a very good chance of having most of the costs of your training met by your local education authority.

The whole question of grants is a very uncertain subject as it not only varies from one local education authority to another, but it also varies with the financial abilities of each individual student.

There is now a government sponsored scheme available from Barclays Bank whereby one can borrow the cost of fees for further education and repay at an advantageous rate after training. Further details can be obtained from any branch of Barclay's Bank.

The second factor to be taken into consideration when considering training is the locality of the college. Most parents would prefer their young people to attend a college near by so that they can still live at home. This is not always possible as many smaller local education authorities do not have a technical college in their area teaching the full beauty therapy courses. The costs of setting up such a department are enormous and many local education authorities do not consider that there is enough demand for trained staff to warrant laying out vast sums of money on setting up a course. The majority of technical colleges, however, do have a hairdressing training department, so often a beauty therapy course, or a part of a beauty therapy course, will be run in that department, or often a combined hairdressing and beauty therapy course. As the City and Guilds of London Institute (C&G) also are an examining body for hairdressing, it was natural for them to see the demand for a combined course and they now offer an examination devoted to the two subjects.

One should start looking for a suitable college by writing to the three examination boards, whose addresses are listed in the appendix. They will send you a list of colleges who are approved by them and are offering courses leading to their examinations. The task then is to contact colleges, either by post or telephone, requesting a prospectus. These will list the courses offered and in most instances will detail the syllabus so that you can decide whether the course is comprehensive enough for your needs.

They will also include details of minimum educational requirements needed for each course. These are usually guide lines only. But be realistic. If the minimum requirement for a course states three GCE 'O' levels or their equivalent, then it is not much point in applying if you do not have even one. The only exceptions to these rules are if you are a mature student. What you obtained when you left school and what you have done in the way of a career since then will be taken into consideration. In these cases the prospective student may be asked to take a small college test designed to see if the person is capable of coping with the course content. This is not so much the practical work but the more intensive theory, particularly the anatomy and physiology and the science aspects.

The next step is to go and see. Obviously you will not be able to visit every college, but choose a few both private and technical to visit. Any college of repute will willingly make an appointment for prospective students to tour the college and discuss the various courses offered. This would not put the student under any obligation to accept a place there if offered.

When viewing a college, both private and technical, you should look carefully at the equipment available for student use. Also ask how many students would be on the course, so that you can ascertain how many would be expecting to use the same equipment. It is a poor college where students have to wait hours to get a chance to use certain items of equipment. The examining boards mentioned all issue equipment lists specifying the type and minimum amount of items a college should have before it undertakes to provide tuition to their syllabus. This list must be strictly adhered to and it is added to from time to time. Examiners who visit each college to undertake the practical examinations on behalf of each examination board have strict instructions to report to the board if colleges do not comply to this minimum standard equipment list. There is also a regular revision of equipment lists to ensure that any new apparatus which has a valid place in a working salon, will be available for student training.

Educational requirements

Regardless of which college you finally choose, be it a local education authority college or a private beauty school, there are certain educational requirements laid down by the examining boards to which the college must comply.

The requirements are changing all the time so the following is only intended as a general guide, and should not be held as hard and fast rules, but usually the courses offered and the educational requirements are as follows:

City and Guilds courses

Course 761-1 The Beauty Therapist's Certificate
In general this course is spread over two years full time instruction. As the student must be over 20 years of age on 1 September of the year in which she intends to take the examination, the usual starting age for this course is 18 years.

Students must have good passes in three subjects, including English and a science subject in the GCE 'O' level ('O' grade in the Scottish Certificate of Education), Grade 1 level in the Certificate of Secondary Education or

Course 761-3 Electrical Epilation Certificate
As the starting age for commencing the 761-3 and the 761-1 courses is 18, obviously the student has to do something between finishing 'O' levels and starting college. Most colleges prefer their students to go on and do an 'A' level in art or science. However, as application must be made to the individual college at or about the time of 'O' levels or their equivalent then college staff will advise a student on what they would prefer them to do. This course 761-3 is restricted to either those students who have already completed a course in beauty therapy or students studying both subjects at the same time. The age and educational requirements remain the same as for the 761-1 Beauty Therapist's Course.

Course 762-1 Manicure Certificate
The selection of students for this course is within the discretion

of the college and no specific educational requirements are stated. This course is usually offered with most City and Guilds Hairdressing courses.

Course 762-3 Cosmetic Make-up
This course is also intended for the Hairdressing student who wishes to obtain a qualification in cosmetic make-up. The selection of students is within the discretion of the college and no specific educational qualifications are required. However, students should either be following, or have successfully completed, a City and Guilds course in hairdressing.

A list of colleges offering these courses can be obtained by writing to the City and Guilds of London Institute whose address can be found in the appendix.

Confederation of International Beauty Therapy and Cosmetology Courses

Beautician Diploma course
Entry requirements are a minimum of three GCE 'O' level passes or their equivalent, one of which must be English and the second preferably human biology or a science subject. Minimum age at examination is $17\frac{1}{2}$ years.

Beauty Therapists Diploma course
Educational entry requirements are the same as the Beauticians Diploma course.

Aestheticienne Diploma course
This is a combination of the two former courses. The entry requirements are the same as for the former and the minimum age at the time of examination is $18\frac{1}{2}$ years.

Electrolysist Diploma course
This course has a minimum of 200 hours of training if included with the Aestheticiennes syllabus, but is extended to 300 hours of training if the candidate has no previous knowledge of the theory essential for this subject. Minimum age requirement is $18\frac{1}{2}$ at time of examination.

Assistant Beautician Diploma course
A course designed for students who will be employed in salons as assistants, or for hairdressers who wish to extend their range of treatments. The minimum age level for this course is $16\frac{1}{2}$ years at date of examination.

A list of colleges, both local education authority and private, offering these courses can be obtained by writing to The Secretariat of the Confederation of International Beauty Therapy and Cosmetology whose address can be found in the appendix of this book.

International Health and Beauty Council courses

The IHBC offers a wider range of courses than the two previously mentioned examination boards, with varying lengths of training and educational requirements. These were designed in this manner so that the complete course could be taken in sections, or modules, enabling a student to study for the complete qualification either consecutively at one time or in smaller modules, one at a time. The latter method is of most benefit to the mature student who has to work between training times, in order to finance her beauty training. The complete course, however, covers the same amount of theoretical knowledge and practical skills and depth of study as the two previously mentioned examination boards syllabuses.

Beauty Consultant's Certificate
This is basically intended for those intending to sell cosmetics. Entry requirement is two GCE 'O' level passes or their equivalent and a minimum age of 18 at the date of examination. Alternatively, the entrant should be taking the course in conjunction with some other approved educational course, or be currently employed in a store by a cosmetic retailer or be employed in a hairdressers or a beauty salon.

Manicure Certificate
Entry requirement is two GCE 'O' level passes or their equivalent and a minimum age of 17 years at the date of

examination. Alternatively the entrant can take the course in conjunction with a hairdressing course.

Make-up Manicure Certificate
Entry requirements are as for the Manicure Certificate.

The Beauty Specialists Diploma
Entry requirements are three passes at GCE 'O' level or their equivalent and a minimum age of 18 years at the time of examination.

The Finnish Sauna Diploma
Entry requirements are three passes at GCE 'O' level or their equivalent, or the entrant should be currently employed in a sauna establishment, public sports centre or beauty salon. Minimum age 18 years.

The Diploma in Health and Beauty
Entry requirements are four passes at GCE 'O' level or their equivalent and a minimum of 18 years.

Certificate in Epilation
Entry requirement is two passes at GCE 'O' level or their equivalent and a minimum age of 18 years. Most colleges stipulate that this certificate can only be taken in conjunction with a facial beauty therapy qualification unless the applicant is SRN or similar.

Diploma in Electrology
Entry requirements are three passes in GCE 'O' level or their equivalent and a minimum of 18 years at examination. Candidates must have completed the course for the Certificate in Epilation or have been exempt therefrom by reason of an alternative acceptable qualification.

The International Beauty Therapist's Diploma
Entry requirements are four passes at GCE 'O' level or their equivalent and a minimum age of 18 years.

The Remedial Camouflage Certificate
Entry requirements are an approved facial beauty therapy qualification and a minimum age of 18 years at examination.

The International Masters Diploma in Health and Beauty
Entry requirements are five passes at GCE 'O' level or their equivalent, but two 'A' level passes are preferred. There is a minimum lower age limit for starting the course and that is 18 years.

The International Beauty Therapy Teacher's Diploma
Entry requirements vary from college to college and application to the college of your choice or to The Director General, IHBC is suggested. This course is obviously reserved for therapists already holding the International Beauty Therapist's Diploma or the Master's Certificate. Some colleges also stipulate that a student applying for teacher training should have had at least five years working experience as a beauty therapist before contemplating this.

The International Health and Beauty Council stress that the details given are the minimum requirements laid down and some colleges may ask for higher levels of qualification in some instances. All IHBC courses are graded and listed by the Burnham Further Education Committee.

International Institute of Sports Therapy

The Sports Massage Certificate
Entry requirement of two passes at GCE 'O' level or their equivalent unless the candidate is currently employed in a sports centre, health club, sports club, public baths or health and sports therapy establishment.

The Health and Sports Therapy Diploma
Entry requirements four passes at GCE 'O' level or their equivalent, including English language and minimum age of 18 at examination. Specific exemption is given if the candidate is employed in a sports centre, sports club, health farm or similar establishment.

International Diploma in Sports Therapy
Entry requirements of two 'A' level GCEs or not less than five 'O' level passes or their equivalent which must include a pass in the language of the country in which the examination is taken, and desirably two science subjects. No exemption from the educational requirements are granted except in the case of other examined qualifications counted as equivalent or approved experience acceptable to the Institute. Their qualification is intended to be for students of mature attitudes and capable of acting in a managerial capacity and the minimum age of 19 years at the day of examination is mandatory.

Further information on any of the courses mentioned or lists of colleges running these courses can be obtained by writing to the International Institute of Sports Therapy at the address listed in the appendix.

Other training

There are many other organisations offering beauty courses, the largest of these being ITEC, details of these courses can be obtained by application to the relevant college teaching to their system or from ITEC itself the address of which appears in the appendix.

Electrolysis training

In the field of electrolysis there are two other professional bodies offering qualifications which are respected in the field. These are The Institute of Electrolysis and the British Association of Electrolysists.

With both organisations there is a syllabus of training laid down with a minimum number of training hours stipulated, particularly as far as the practical lessons are concerned. Some beauty colleges will also offer courses leading to examination with either of these two professional organisations as well as the others already stated. Further details of both can be found in the appendix.

Student days

Right from the beginning of training the student beauty therapist is encouraged to collect her own small equipment for use during practical sessions. Manicure equipment, eyebrow tweezers, make-up brushes and many other small items can be collected and carried to practical classes by the student. As with the professionally qualified therapist, the student must learn the importance of building up her own range of skin-care products and cosmetics. The problems of transporting these items can be overcome by buying some container which can be carried upright in order not to spill the contents. A new student will find that individual college lecturers have a favourite container ranging from either the more expensive professional make-up cases to the more simple versions such as the baby boxes sold by Mothercare.

This box then becomes invaluable to the student as it contains all the tools and materials necessary for her to practise her new found skills. In beauty therapy the old maxim 'practise makes perfect' certainly applies. Students will be actively encouraged to practise on any willing member of the family or friends.

Traditionally the therapist wears a white dress and this the student has to supply for herself. As most colleges insist on all their students wearing the same pattern dress it is usually arranged for the girls to purchase them through the college. Some colleges also insist on the wearing of pale stockings or tights and white shoes. These the student must purchase herself.

With all colleges the emphasis will be placed on good grooming with the beauty therapy student always looking the part with her hair neatly styled and her own personal make-up expertly applied. Beauty students at mixed discipline colleges can usually be spotted instantly in a crowd as they stand out because of their impeccable grooming. Many beauty therapy lecturers have a morning 'parade' before lectures begin, particularly if the day's timetable includes a practical session in which members of the general public act as models. Any student appearing dishevelled or ungroomed in any way would be sent to the cloakroom to put matters right. It may appear fussy, but first impressions matter and the student therapist must learn this.

On the completion of the training the student will be required to sit a series of examinations set by the boards. These are usually conducted on a national system, with every college participating taking the examinations on the same day. The written papers are sometimes essay type questions and occasionally multiple choice questions. Practical examinations are also scheduled with an independent examiner visiting the college and observing the students performing a specified list of practical skills. She may re-inforce her opinion of a student's work by asking a few questions.

After college: scholarships

Most students after college set about the daunting task of finding employment but for at least one girl a year, there is a whole twelve months of exploring the exciting world of the retailing and treatment side of beauty therapy in the form of a scholarship.

In 1985 Clarins (UK) Ltd decided to arrange a scholarship to enable at least one young therapist to gain valuable experience with their company in the art and skills of assessing a client's needs and matching that need with products from their range.

It is called the **Clarins/Cidesco Scholarship** and is open to any student who qualifies for a Cidesco Diploma. A panel of senior people in the industry are invited to interview the candidates on several occasions. The scholarship guarantees a year of intensive work experience and further training, helping to add to her skills by adding a commercial aspect to her already technical training. Part of the year is spent in Britain under the direct guidance of Lesley Wooley, the technical training manager, and part spent in France at the headquarters of the Clarins Company.

Perhaps other large companies may follow the lead Clarins have set by realising the value that a well trained beauty therapist can be to their company if she firmly believes in the quality and integrity of their products.

Specialised training: television make-up artists

The training structure for a television make-up artist follows quite a different pattern from the rest of the beauty world. Theirs is such a specialised subject that it is done at the studios themselves. The brief outline of training covered here refers throughout to the requirements for BBC television. The Independent Television companies are very much the same and their training schedules also, but anyone interested should contact the company direct.

The BBC receives literally thousands of applications every year so they can be very selective when choosing people to train as make-up artists. To begin with, they advertise any vacancies for trainees in two publications, *The Stage* and *The Listener*. Applicants are then sent forms to complete, and provided they have the educational background required they may be short-listed for an interview.

Applicants must be at least $20\frac{1}{2}$ years old with 'A' level passes in subjects such as art, history and English. They must have then either obtained a City and Guilds of London Institute Certificate in hairdressing or followed an art course to degree level, taking hair and make-up as an extra curricula subject.

When trained the BBC make-up artist would be working in the main studios in London or in one of the provincial cities such as Belfast, Glasgow, Manchester, Birmingham, Cardiff or Bristol. However, all initial training takes place in London where the new recruit joins the course as a trainee make-up assistant. She will be under constant supervision as learning goes on much longer than the initial set training period, but as she acquires new skills, she can rise to grades in between and then finally to Senior Make-up Artist. It would probably take about five years to rise to Make-up Artist and it is a highly competitive field.

During her work, the trainee make-up assistant would be supervised constantly by a make-up artist and together they would be expected to cover a whole range of different programme needs, ranging from news programmes and chat shows to full scale drama series.

Many of these would require an 'in depth' knowledge of the fashions in hairstyle and make up of a certain period in history. The make-up artist is responsible for the hair and wigs of the artists as well as their facial make-up. That is why a hairdressing qualification is more important than a beauty therapy one.

Working with famous people and stars, who might be extremely nervous or temperamental, calls for some very special qualities. The selection board therefore are looking for trainees who are adaptable, cool, calm and capable, yet can be friendly and at ease with people from all walks of life.

The working hours are very erratic, which means the BBC TV make-up artist has a very restricted social life. They certainly must love their work to put up with these conditions but, on the credit side, it would not be described as a boring job. Meeting famous people face to face and realising that millions of people are looking at your work must be very rewarding. Although not strictly a beauty therapist it is the kind of application of skills that might appeal to some. See also pages 56 and 57.

3 Extending your knowledge and your horizons

The first post

Armed with the new skills you have learned at college, the task now is to find that first post as a beauty therapist. As in all other types of work, there are areas of unemployment, but perseverance usually wins through. The newly qualified therapist often finds herself in a 'catch 22' situation, where employers are asking for someone with at least one year's experience. How can you get that valuable experience if nobody is prepared to take you on the staff? The secret is to keep trying, someone will eventually. The kind of establishment most likely to take you without any experience is one of the larger firms that have more staff. There you can be placed under the guidance of a more experienced therapist who will guide you through the pitfalls of your early days until you are confident to work alone.

Most good colleges encourage their students to explore every angle of the profession to decide which type of establishment is most suited to the individual. Often visits are arranged to health clubs, health farms, beauty salons and similar establishments, in an attempt to match the individual student to a suitable environment. Many also arrange for their students to gain valuable work experience with local employers in the profession. This gives the student an insight into the problems experienced when one is actually doing the work for hours on end. The majority of students comment after work experience, that they had not realised how quickly the therapist has to work despite any number of distractions going on around her. Another frequent remark is about the large amount of cleaning and very mundane jobs which have to be done in the general routine of a busy day. All these things cannot be envisaged by the student who learns only within the four walls of a classroom.

Matching the skills

The experienced beauty therapy tutor not only teaches the manual skills needed but also she watches and assesses all of her pupils and can easily match the student to the most suitable form of work for her. Many different things will affect the choices you have to make before applying for a post. A student who is already married and has home commitments will obviously find it difficult to cope with working in an establishment which is not within daily reach of her home. Also the student who much prefers the city and night life would be most unwise to apply for a post in a health farm. These are usually sited in the heart of the countryside, for obvious reasons, and the staff find very little in the way of entertainment.

The student who shows a marked affinity for exercising and body treatments should combine the two and look for a vacancy in a health club or gymnasium. On the other hand, if electrolysis is your best skill, then there will be no difficulty for you to find a place in any high street beauty salon. Often it will be a case of taking any job that is offered in the first place just to gain that all important experience. Then you can specialise and try all the different facets of this very exciting profession.

Applying for a post

A careful watch on the classified section of the local newspaper may find you a position vacant in your local area. The local job centre will willingly take all your particulars and put you in touch with any prospective employers. If the area in which you have chosen to work does not contain many salons then you may have to be a bit more adventurous yourself and go looking a bit harder. A copy of your local *Yellow Pages* directory and copies of those of areas to which you could commute, will soon show you a list of all the various health and beauty establishments in your area. A neatly written or preferably typed letter of application, together with a self addressed envelope for a reply, should be sent to all of them.

Hopefully, if they do not require staff just at this time, they may interview you and keep your name and address on file for any future vacancy.

Curriculum vitae

Most colleges instruct their students how to prepare a CV as it is known. This is a resumé of your career so far and all other relevant pieces of information about yourself. This should be prepared in a business-like manner stating information such as your age, your school, where you live now and if you are married or single.

Follow this information with the most important information that any prospective employer will want to know, that is all the beauty courses you have taken, all the results, pass fail or credits and distinction, and then the name of the college where you studied. It is not enough to say you studied beauty at the X College of Beauty. Not all prospective employers know the precise details of a college course, but if you tell them the exact nature of the course and the examinations taken, then they are fully in the picture.

Many college lecturers suggest putting down everything that you do, hobbies, etc. Sorry to disagree but most employers are not interested in what time of night you walk the dog on the common. They would be very interested to know, however, that you have a driving licence and can speak two other languages. List your hobbies if they are relevant, but do not omit one little detail about your college studies. They are the most important.

It will also help a prospective employer to know exactly when you would be free to take up this new appointment. She may be stuck with someone leaving quite suddenly, so if you can say that you are free to start at any time, it may help clinch the job for you.

The interview

This may all sound like common sense but it is surprising how many would-be employees ignore these very ordinary aspects of an interview. If the salon is some distance away and in a place which is quite unfamiliar to you, there are two plans of action. Either ask the person granting you the interview to send you or dictate over the phone, detailed instructions of how to find it, or go a few days earlier, possibly with a friend, and find out exactly where it is so that on the great day you can arrive looking smart and unhurried because you have already had the sense to establish just where to go and also how long it will take to reach the salon.

Even if you normally dress very casually, please make the effort to appear reasonably smartly dressed. With older employers, certainly it does make a good impression. Please give great attention to your own make-up, remember it will possibly be a beauty therapist interviewing you. Speak up clearly because she is looking for someone who is going to speak clearly and pleasantly to her customers, and good luck!

The job is yours!

Do ensure, before you accept the job that has been offered to you, that the conditions of employment are fully explained to you. By law the employer has to give each employee a contract of employment which sets out in writing all details such as hours to be worked, pay for those hours, pay for overtime, if any. How many days holiday you will be entitled to, and if you have to provide your own white dress overalls.

Make sure you know exactly what time you start and then ask if you may come in a few hours on a day before you begin seeing clients so that you may familiarise yourself with the salon layout. It would be awful to go in the first morning and leave the client two or three times to ask where the cotton wool and creams are kept. Most good employers would not book you a client for the first hour on your first day, but some may.

Working abroad

All these things seem fairly straight forward if the post one has applied for is in Britain, but you can hardly go and take a look at the place if it is thousands of miles overseas. Most overseas advertisers will state that interviews will take place in Britain. It would be most foolish to accept a post abroad if one had not seen or spoken to one's prospective employer or their agent in Britain. Even if such an interview does take place it is as well to have a colleague or older member of your family with you, just to confirm all that has been said.

At an interview, all the same things as you would ask at a British salon would have to be asked as well as some which are more important. Firstly one has to ask for some documentary evidence that the salon and the employer actually do exist. This must be checked with the embassy of that country here in London who should be able to authenticate this information. Do not attempt to travel to the country unless this has been done. The next thing is to get quite clear information about the costs of the flight out and back, and who pays for that? Normally your new employer will, but what happens if (a) you are not suitable to them or (b) you do not like working conditions or the country and you want to come home? Who pays the air fare then?

Ask about salary and how it is going to be paid. Ask what the current exchange rate is and see if it is going to be worth your while to go. Ask if you will be paying income tax in that country or does their country allow foreign nationals to be tax free? Remember if you take up full time employment abroad and you only return for normal holidays in Britain, you may be able to be classified non-taxable in Britain. Tax is always a tricky business so you should call at the local income tax office and find out before you consider taking the big step.

Another must is to find out if one has to have a visa and a work permit for the country in question. Once again the embassy of the country will be able to give you all that and also a lot of background information about the country and its customs and, more importantly, about its laws. Many middle eastern countries have strict laws about the consumption of alcohol, or the manner of women's dress. Because you don't agree with these ideas, doesn't mean that you can ignore them. You will find that many countries are not so lenient with people who break their laws as we are in Britain.

All this talk must not put you off from applying for a post overseas however. Many therapists have found themselves really good employment overseas and have been a great deal more financially rewarded than those that have stayed at home. It just means that you must take more care, and be more alert to the possibility of dangers than you have when applying for a post at home.

One final word on an overseas appointment. Before going please buy a phrase book and learn to say, at least, please and thank you in the language of that country. You may be reassured by the person interviewing you that everyone speaks English, but if it is not the natural tongue of that country then do try to learn just a few phrases. It is sure to create a good impression if one can only be polite.

Where are you going to apply first?

The traditional beauty salon

In the early days of the profession, the traditional beauty salon was the only place in which one could receive treatment. They existed mainly in London and the larger cities and it was through the pioneer work done by them that the profession flourished and expanded into the skilled and technical career that it is today.

Now to be found in every small town and even in village high streets, the beauty salon is as familiar a sight as the local hairdressing salon. Most of them remain exclusively beauty but with the addition of an expanding retail sales side. The majority are still owner managed by a qualified therapist who employs others to help her. They usually offer a full range of treatments along with electrolysis, which is often considered to be the 'bread and butter' of the salon. The student that chooses to apply for this kind of work will be expected to have several good qualities. The first will be versatility. With only a few therapists on the staff, it will be imperative that the newcomer is able to perform every treatment offered at the salon.

To be able to work to time is another asset required. The appointment book will be so finely dovetailed for time that it will be essential that the new therapist is, not only capable of performing the treatment properly, but also within the allotted time. It will not only be because another client will be waiting but also, if the space is limited, the room or cubicle may be needed by another therapist. Some salons are equipped with rooms or cubicles containing all machinery and materials required to perform the whole range of treatments offered. Others, however, may have different rooms or cubicles for the various types of treatments. This, of course, cuts down the expense of equipment but means that the therapists move from room to room according to the treatment booked. This method of working demands a great deal of concentration when making appointments. Care must be taken to ensure that not only is the therapist free, but also the room or cubicle containing the equipment.

If the salon is a good one, then the new therapist can expect to be very busy, with certain times of the year being busier than others. The early months of the year are body orientated. Most clients having over indulged at Christmas and New Year, follow up their New Year resolutions to get slim by booking up for most of the figure treatments. Also this time of the year is in the party season so make-up and manicures are still very much in demand. As the year progresses, the demand for sun-beds steps up and the waxing boom begins, although, like electrolysis, waxing is now in demand the whole year through. Traditionally the salons usually have a quiet October, although nobody really knows why. Then the pressure builds up again towards Christmas with nearly all of the treatments being in great demand. The wise salon owner also increases her retail sales stock at this time and usually sells gift vouchers for treatments. If the salon is large enough to have a receptionist then the sales will probably be her exclusive province, but most of these type of salons offer a bonus incentive scheme to the therapist if she sells both retail lines and courses of treatments. It is difficult to generalise, but most pay a basic wage as well as these sales incentive bonus schemes.

The most important person in this type of salon, as in any other, is the client. Most expect their therapists to be quiet, charming, and a good listener. As there are not many other staff employed the new therapist will be expected to build up her own client list from casual clients who come for the first time. Although she must be prepared to be interchangeable and take over another therapists clients during periods of holidays or illness. The hours in the traditional beauty salon are normally quite easy with possibly one or two late nights to be worked.

If you think you would like to be working very set hours, in the same place, with a steady supply of the same clients, where you could build up a reputation for good work, then this is your kind of establishment.

Beauty in a department store

This is basically a variation on the former style of working, except in this instance, the owners are invariably a large company with 'in store' salons in two or three chains of the large retail department stores. In this type of salon the list of treatments offered are usually more limited and very uniform with the therapists working strictly to a routine laid down by head office. Work will be supervised by a manageress who in turn is answerable to an area director. The work would be the same in the Blackpool salon as it is in the Birmingham one. This makes life easier for the new therapist who sometimes is taken on as a locum. This means moving from town to town, filling in for holiday or illness absences of the regular therapist. Usually, if the therapist proves to be efficient and adaptable, she will be offered the first vacancy that arises. The salary is normally very basic with sales incentives as before, but many also enjoy the privileges given to the staff of the department store, that of buying goods at staff discount.

The hours are usually the same as the store so are not usually too anti-social.

Beauty room in a hairdressers

Some people consider this to be the most obvious place for a beauty salon to be. This is fine if the hairdressing salon is a more traditional one but not so good if it is one of the modern, very noisy establishments. Clients may like noise and lots of activity when having their hair done, but much prefer privacy and quietness when it comes to their beauty treatments. There are also limitations on the clients who come for treatment as they are usually only those who are visiting the hairdressers. It can, therefore, be very restricting if a new therapist gets herself a good reputation in the area but new clients are hesitant about coming for treatments in case they are expected to break their loyalty to their present hairdresser. It very much depends on who owns the salon. It also depends on how much space is available. Many such beauty rooms only provide a limited range of treatments, mainly the more popular, such as make-up, facials, waxing, eyelash tinting and manicures.

Often the owner will not be a therapist so the new therapist has to be prepared to work under her own direction. Many such salons are seeing the wisdom of employing staff who have both hairdressing and beauty therapy qualifications. This makes them very employable. This idea has been taken up by many local education authority colleagues who often offer a combined hairdressing/beauty therapy course. Pay is usually about the same as the stylists in the hair salon, and incentive schemes will probably be in operation. There will be plenty of working companionship from the hair stylists which may suit the student who might miss the camaraderie of student days at college.

The hours are usually those of the hair salon with several late nights being worked. There are, however, the usual staff benefits of free or cheaper hairdressing, etc.

The newly qualified beauty therapist should avoid any scheme which offers rent-a-chair facilities. These are being widely advertised these days, but are full of too many pitfalls for the newly qualified. Wait until you have at least one or two years' experience of working for other people before branching out on your own, particularly with this type of agreement.

Beauty in a health club

In the last few years there has been a mushroom growth of excellent health clubs throughout the country. Most large cities can boast at least one if not two. These are modelled on the lines of the traditional health farm but are situated in very built up areas where there is a large population from which they draw their membership. The other difference is, of course, they do not provide sleeping facilities, but nearly all the other things associated with health farms, such as heated swimming pools, hydrotherapy baths, a gymnasium (usually with a very comprehensive selection of circuit weight training equipment), sunbeds, saunas, a beauty room, and often restaurant facilities as well. Many are also offering consultation facilities for alternative medical therapies. The clients generally have to buy a yearly membership which gives access to most of the facilities free. Some have a variation where extras like sun-bed treatments have to be paid for separately. With almost all of them, the services of the beauty room have to be paid for as an extra and are not included in the yearly membership. Some of them are exclusively for women but many of them have both male and female members usually with different days being scheduled as being male or female. The largest majority of these clubs are run very strictly on a professional basis and it is not usual to find female staff being asked to do treatments on males.

Working hours in this case are going to be very flexible with the new therapist finding that she is asked to do shift work often until late in the evening, depending on which department she is employed in. Those who have the ability to supervise and plan circuit weight training schedules are very much in demand and will find that they often will be in the section which works latest. The beauty room is the one which tends to follow normal working hours.

This is the most likely employment for a student straight from college. Working under the supervision of a more experienced person or of the manageress herself, she will gain invaluable experience. With the very large membership that most clubs have, it is difficult to establish a clientele that are asking exclusively for you. However, with more staff than usual, working conditions are usually very good. Pay tends to be average and sometimes a bit under as clubs are aware that they can pick up girls from college all the time so there does tend to be a quick turn over in staff.

Beauty in a sports centre

Just as there has been this rapid growth in the private health club so has there been a similar growth in the local authority owned sports centres. Relaxation on the rates has been an innovation of the eighties, which has caught the imagination of the general public. More so since everyone seems to be health and fitness conscious at the moment. This has resulted in a great demand for these centres to offer more and more of the facilities which are available in the private gyms and clubs. Some have the traditional beauty room while others do not. Those that do are often offered out on a rental basis for the therapist to become self-employed. Once again, hours are going to be rather anti-social as their busiest times are when working people have finished and want to relax. Any student who is very fit and interested in a number of sporting activities would be ideally suited to this area of work. Working conditions are basically the same as the private health club, although surprisingly, the salary is usually higher because you would be employed by the local authority who pays to an accepted national scale.

The equipment and the surroundings are not always as luxurious as that of the private clubs, but it depends very much on the age of the place and the area in which it is situated.

Health and beauty farms

Health farms, or health hydros, as they prefer to be called, have retained their popularity over the years as a very expensive form of getting oneself fit. Their prices charged usually reflect the standard of luxury one can expect to find. Normally situated in a magnificent country house, they offer their guests the benefits of a superb health and fitness club combined with the surroundings of a first class hotel. The British ones have always enjoyed the reputation of being of high standards which means they are very often frequented by wealthy overseas guests as well as British. Working conditions are quite good but as with most hotel staff, private accommodation is not available so be prepared to share your sleeping quarters with at least one or two other girls on the staff.

Working conditions are long and hard, but with a change of clientele every week or two. Again, whatever you show an aptitude for, usually determines in which department you would be mainly working, although in these establishments, staff must be prepared to be very flexible and substitute for each other as and when the need arises. After work tends to be just as enjoyable, because you have friends and colleagues with whom you share your spare time as well as your working hours. Although situated in the country, most employees find their time there most enjoyable. Each establishment varies so it is very difficult to generalise but most pay average or below average wages. Once again, staff straight from college are not difficult to find and provided that they maintain a good managerial staff level, a rapid turnover in staff is not such a drastic occurrence as in other salons; however, a good form of work in which to gain work experience, particularly if you like meeting the rich and famous.

Beauty at sea

If you have a desire to travel then working as a beauty therapist on one of the luxurious ocean cruise ships might be the answer. The well-established companies that run these salon at sea are very strict about the staff they accept. They are not the slightest bit interested in anyone who has not had at least a few years' experience. They much prefer the girl who has spent at least three years gaining valuable client handling experience at a health farm or similar establishment. The type of clients encountered on the luxury liners are the same as those of the health farm, with the emphasis being on the more demanding nature of some of the foreign passengers.

Another ability they are looking for is someone who can work tidily in a small confined space. Ships salons are usually very compact, and on some lines they are autonomous but on others they come under the direct managership of the hairdressing salon.

Anyone who takes this job must, once again, be prepared to work long hours with your time on board being very hectic. The reward for all this hard work is above average pay, long holidays when the ship is in port or doing a turn around somewhere, and of course to see exotic parts of the world. It is a demanding type of career with your social life being strictly limited to the other crew members. Fraternising with passengers is frowned on. The types of treatments performed are similar to elsewhere but very much guided by strict head office rulings. Although you are employed by the parent company, anyone on board be it crew, staff, or passengers are under the direction of the Ship's Captain. Normally a uniform is supplied and in some respects you will be treated as crew.

Unlike the health farm where the clients change every one or two weeks, the cruise usually lasts longer than that so be prepared to face the same clients day after day. The sea-going therapist must, therefore, be happy about leaving home, and also not suffer from travel or sea-sickness. With all the passengers around, paying for attention, nobody has time to cope with a seasick, homesick therapist. Although, should you be ill during the voyage, you would, of course, have the benefit of treatment from the ship's medical team exactly the same as anyone else.

Most girls who choose this form of work, like it very much and usually stay in the job for about 5 to 7 years.

Television and film make-up artist

A career that is as far removed from that of either the health farm or the luxury liner is that of the television and film make-up artist. Their work can vary from the very routine and ordinary work of daily disguising minor facial imperfections such as a too florid skin or a shiny bald head for people who are appearing on news or interview shows, to that of being out on location, freezing cold, soaking wet, trying to keep up a continuity of make-up on actors and actresses who are equally cold and wet and very disgruntled about having to shoot a scene again for the umpteenth time.

However glamorous their work may appear to be, that is not the way most of them describe it, and yet they all seem to be dedicated to it. The training is very specialised and has been detailed in chapter two, but it must be stressed that it is a highly competitive career with both BBC and Independent Television companies getting thousands of applications per year. This is the area for which the very small percentage of male students who enter beauty therapy seem to aim. See pages 42 and 43.

Electrolysis clinics

A great contrast to the work of the television make-up artist is that of the therapist that devotes her time exclusively to the finely detailed work of the **electrologist**. To do this one has to acquire the very specialised skill of delicately probing accurately and the other necessary skill of client handling. The psychological aspect of this work is very important and many students who take it as part of their course feel that they cannot cope with this work when actually confronted with it in salon practice. It requires a very special aptitude and is often more suited to the maturer therapist.

There are several companies who specialise in clinics which offer only electrolysis and these are an ideal starting place for the student who feels she would be happy dedicating her work to this branch of the art. It is necessary, however, to make sure at your interview that your ideas and theories about the work are the same as the company policy or you may find that you are very unhappy, believing one thing and actually having to tell the clients something different. The working hours are about the same as any high street salon with the wages offered being about average.

Technical representatives

Companies supplying both equipment and materials and cosmetics find that they need someone with a beauty qualification to call on salon owners to sell their products. The technical sales representative needs not only to be able to sell, but also be able to discuss products, their use in treatment programmes, the technicalities of the various machines, and also to be able to demonstrate the equipment effectively.

The companies are usually looking for someone who has had some salon experience but in some cases may be prepared to take a student straight from college. However, as the people to whom she will be selling – the salon owners, are usually more mature people she will have to be self-confident and able to speak up and converse well with people. The work involves a lot of driving so obviously a driving licence is essential, although most firms provide a car, so your own car is not always necessary. Initially some time would have to be spent at the companies headquarters for briefing sessions and for intensive training in the use of their particular brands.

A very confident, well groomed therapist with the ability to organise herself and her daily work schedule is needed for this kind of work. In return the companies offer a very good salary and often the use of the car for personal use at weekends. Grooming allowances are often given as well as staff discounts and bonus schemes. If all this seems to be too good to be true, just think a little. It is not easy to drive miles through bad weather, find a place to park in strange towns, hop in and out of the car, carry a heavy sample case and still appear on someone's door step looking neat and tidy and hopefully glamorous. Even if you do, the odds are that you have chosen the day that the salon is closed, or that the owner takes the day off!

Beauty on wheels

A recently reported survey carried out by an equipment manufacturer discovered that, two years ago, 15% of all college leaving beauty therapy students interviewed, were planning to set up a mobile beauty therapy service. Asking the same questions of a similar random group this year showed that about 60% were now planning to enter the profession in this way. Traditionally this has always been a method of building up a nucleus of a clientele list. After a few years, however, the majority of visiting therapists decide that they have had enough and most of them find premises in the area in which their clients' live. This means that when they open the doors of their first salon, they have a ready made clientele who will make the effort to come to the salon out of loyalty.

It is, of course, a reasonably inexpensive way of becoming self-employed but it can still be quite a big step for the beginner. The largest expense, if one is not already available, is that of a car. An old banger will not do. If you are offering a service to the public, then that service must be reliable so a car that starts every time and is one hundred per cent dependable is a must. Also the car must be a hatch back or estate car so that equipment can easily be placed in and out of the car.

Most types of equipment can be purchased in a transportable form and have been designed for just this occasion. It can then be used quite well in a salon when the time eventually comes. However, it is the odd things that tend to cause annoyance. Wax pots have the awful habit of spilling if you have to pull up quickly. Client's beds are usually too low to use for treatment so a portable couch or chair is a must. This can be quite a weight to heave in and out of the car. The lighting is not always as good as it could be so a portable light and magnifier are essential.

Another aspect of this type of work is that the therapist must be a very orderly and disciplined person. Nothing could be worse for both the client or the therapist than if she has to keep stopping in the middle of a treatment to go out to the car for something she needs!

While on the point of discipline, the appointment book would have to be kept with the same organisation and care. The area roughly covered would need to be divided up and a day a week allotted to each area, with as many clients as possible being attended to in that one area. It would be economically unsound to spend large amounts of the day travelling between clients or going back over the same ground each day. Traffic hold ups, road diversions and generally heavy traffic can cause chaos to a carefully planned visiting therapist's appointment book. While the therapist is out all day, there must either be someone to answer the telephone or a good reliable answering machine.

The prices you charge will have to have all these time wasting elements written into them. However, the profit ratio of the fees charged will, of course, be much higher because you will not have the expense of rent, rates, lighting and heating, that a salon would have to cover. Take care that financial records are kept very accurately with all receipts for petrol, car mainte-nance and even pay and display parking slips, being kept for the accountant to assess your profit for submission to the Inland Revenue for tax purposes.

Regrettably a sinister word of warning: do ensure that if you choose this type of work, you also choose your clients carefully, and always be on your guard on a first visit to a new client. A young therapist is very vulnerable if she has been lured to the premises on false pretences, which has happened!

Anyone who has studied the combined Hairdressing and Beauty Therapy course would probably find that offering both mobile beauty therapy and hairdressing maximises their chances of building up a thriving business by this method, especially if they choose an area which does not have a large amount of beauty and hairdressing services in it, particularly in scattered rural areas.

Teaching Beauty Therapy

For a therapist with at least five years' experience in all aspects of salon work, the job of a beauty lecturer or tutor in beauty therapy is an attraction. A good working therapist does not always make a good teacher, and in many instances a good teacher does not necessarily make a good therapist. If you feel you have the ability to do both then it is a good idea to look for training in teaching. The principal beauty therapy organis-ations offer teaching certificates which are acceptable to both private and some technical colleges. Others may prefer their prospective lecturers to hold the City and Guilds of London Further Education Teachers' Training Certificate. Courses leading to the examination for this certificate are run by technical colleges in most areas, usually part time and often in the evenings, or on day release. It may take a couple of years to get through the course studying part time, but it is well worth doing if you intend to make teaching your career.

Once you have acquired your teaching certificate you must start looking for a post. It will be most unlikely that you will immediately find a full-time teaching job, particularly if you are settled in one area and do not want to move. However, write to all the colleges, both private and technical that have a beauty therapy department, that are within motoring distance of your home. You will find that one may offer you a few hours part-time teaching. Take it! This is the only way to build up the all important college experience so that when a full time post does become available you are much more likely to be considered for it.

The beauty journalist

Therapists who feel they have a way with words often look for an opening as a beauty journalist. Although they have such a tremendous influence over their readership the beauty journalist is rarely a trained beauty therapist. First and foremost she must be a trained journalist, and if she has a beauty qualification, all the better, but editors will very rarely accept anyone who is not a qualified journalist.

Although they may not have a beauty qualification, most of them make it their business to find out all they can about the work. They then should be able to write very informed and balanced articles on all aspects of beauty, and many salons find they have a steady supply of clients looking for treatments they have first heard about when reading an article in a magazine. Electrolysis, waxing, and galvanic facials have all gained in popularity following excellent reports about these treatments in magazine articles.

If the need to write burns in you, there is always the local free paper or the church magazine which may like an article on beauty, but there is not much chance of making a career out of it.

Beauty Therapy abroad

So far all the work opportunities discussed have applied to the United Kingdom with the exception of working on the cruise liners but many newly qualified therapists may think of working abroad.

Just a glance through the pages of *Health and Beauty Salon* magazine will show you that there are many British beauty therapists setting up beauty establishments in places such as Spain, Portugal and the West Indies. Sometimes they advertise for British trained staff but often they are obliged by the laws of this country to offer the posts in the first place to therapists who are native to that country.

Unemployment is world wide, so it is equally as difficult, if not more so, to step straight into an overseas post. However, don't let that deter you if you are determined to work abroad. A good British beauty therapy qualification is respected in many countries overseas but that does not mean that they are accepted in every country. Indeed many countries will only recognise their own qualification and quite a few countries have much stricter business and employment regulations than are at present in force in Britain.

Working in the European Economic Community

Theoretically it should be very easy to anyone from an EEC country to obtain work anywhere within the Community. However, in practice, this is not the case. First there is the language barrier. Although English is now the accepted international language, not all people understand it, let alone speak it. Indeed why should they? They have a perfectly good language of their own and are quite happy with it. So do not even contemplate working in a country that speaks another language unless you can either speak that language very well or are prepared to do some intensive study until you can.

Then there is the question of rules and regulations. Did you know that in several European countries you cannot practise electrolysis without a medical qualification? To obtain this kind of information regarding a specific country and details of work permits, one should either write to or call at the embassy for that country. Your local job centre or citizens advice bureau will supply you with the addresses of these.

Most of the European countries have an excellent beauty therapy training scheme so that any vacancies for staff are usually filled by their own students. However, a letter of application to the embassy of the country of your choice will give you all the necessary information.

Working in the Middle East

The term Middle East covers not only a large geographic area but also a collection of countries with vastly different cultures and creeds, from the very sophisticated nations whose women are as liberated as those in the west, to very poor primitive countries in which the women are very little more than possessions of their husbands or fathers. In recent years the more liberated women have been able to study beauty therapy themselves so there are a number of salons and schools in some of the countries, but in others there are only a few salons, usually as part of a department store or similar establishment, where foreign nationals have been able to obtain posts as therapists.

However, it is unusual for foreign nationals to be able to own their own premises or sometimes even to hold managerial positions. Most middle eastern countries insist on their own people either owning or at least having a partnership in any business venture which involves foreign nationals.

Usually in these countries there is a great division between poor and rich with only women from the families of the latter being able to afford treatment. Over 90% of the cosmetics and treatment creams used in these countries are imported from

America, France and Britain. Cheaper brands are not popular, as they tend to think if something isn't expensive it isn't good.

In nearly every middle eastern culture the colour of the skin can vary from almost as dark as the African negro to a much paler tone. The intense sun has an extremely drying effect on the skin so any skin-care treatment or range of cosmetics which will help retard the ageing process is very well received. The sun also tends to make the skin very greasy which could become very troublesome and spotty if neglected.

In the more liberated nations the women wear make-up but it tends to be much less than in this country although it is usually very well applied. Some of the more strictly religious countries forbid the wearing of make-up at all, so all salon work in those countries would be restricted to skin-care treatments. As with women the whole world over, the middle eastern woman is very interested in her figure. Traditionally women of the Arabic race have always been beautifully slim when young but tend to put weight on after marriage and childbirth. Therefore figure control and dieting clinics are very popular, especially as a large number of them wear western clothes which show up a bad figure much more than do their traditional garments.

Marriages are still arranged in some of the countries, especially among the wealthier families. The brides are very young and the wedding costume is bright and gaudy compared to the western tradition of wearing white. It is fascinating, however, to be called to do a wedding make-up in these cases. As in Britain the young women who experiment with different clothes and louder make-up are regarded as looking 'tarty' by their elders.

It is interesting for a beauty therapist to see many of the ancient beauty arts still being practised to this day and quite effectively in some cases. Many women still use the time honoured Arabic way of removing excess hair by heating honey and mixing it with other ingredients until it is a toffee-like consistency and then rolling it over the skin. The hairs are removed as easily as with our modern soft hair removal waxes. There is also an ancient method of removing hair by working over it with a fine cotton loop and virtually tieing a slipknot over each hair and pulling it out. This may sound whimsical to western ears but it is still used effectively.

If you do consider working in one of these countries then the embassy of that country will give you all the necessary information. Please do not think because you are British that you can disregard the laws of that country if you don't happen to agree with them. Many middle eastern countries have a law which forbids the drinking of alcohol in their country. You may not agree with it but it would be extremely foolish to think that you could disregard it. Also some countries have strict laws about women's dress, so unless you are prepared to conform, don't consider working in that country. It is highly unlikely that you could break the law by not knowing about it as the British Embassy in that country always makes sure that newcomers are aware of the laws of the land.

Beauty the American way

We would need the whole of this book on this subject alone if we tried to unravel the hundred and one details of working in the world of beauty in the United States of America.

Each of the individual American states has laws of its own governing the working regulations as well as the health codes of the beauty salon. In some states you may only practise if you hold their state qualification but in others some of the more general qualifications as well as the good British ones are accepted.

Most beauty salons are combined with both hairdressing and beauty therapy, but in the majority of them the beauty therapy ends to be restricted to facials and manicures with a lot of emphasis on nail treatments and the application of false nails. Body treatments are usually confined to body therapy clinics and in some states electrical body treatments, such as faradism, are not allowed to be performed without a registered medical practitioner being present on the premises.

It is such a vast geographical land mass that the type of treatments offered would vary from place to place as much as the temperature. Cities in the North and East are very similar in weather conditions to some of our own, whereas in the South and West they experience really tropical conditions. This would of course affect the needs of the clients.

A letter of enquiry to the American Embassy in London would bring you all the information you need, but competition is very fierce with a work permit and visa required.

Beauty Down Under

Australia is comprised of seven states, and although governed by a federal government, they have rules and regulations on employment, health, education and similar things, administered by their own state government. Australia is fast becoming a highly sophisticated country and the women are as liberated and educated as the men. Each state has its own beauty education programme and there are plenty of good colleges, both private and state, teaching beauty therapy. They have many beauty salons but they also have plenty of well qualified Australian staff to fill them. Australia still has a great migrant population from Europeans to Orientals to support so work is not very easy to find.

As in America, Australia has a vast range of country with an enormous temperature range. The southern states are more moderate but the more northern states experience tropical conditions. Even in the south though, the sun has a very drying effect on the skin so any form of skin treatment which can counteract this is very popular. The beauty salons are very British in style and layout and so are their types of treatment courses.

Unfortunately many Britons in the past have gone to Australia with the attitude that they are doing the Australians a favour by going there. They are a warm, welcoming race, but if you take that attitude they will soon show you the door. It is a fascinating and exciting country in which to work and live, if only for a few years, but be prepared to change your outlook on life when you get there.

A letter of enquiry to Australia House in London will bring you the information you need but be prepared for a disappointment. The Secretary of the Australian Federation based in Brisbane has said that they get approximately six letters a week from British beauty therapists requesting jobs in Australia.

Beauty in the Far East

As with the Middle East, the term the Far East covers a multitude of different countries, cultures and creeds. Each has its own traditional ways of education and employment. In many of the countries English is accepted as the international language but working in any of the countries would necessitate learning the language. The need in some of the far eastern countries tends to be for trained beauty therapy lecturers rather than therapists. Most of the countries have strict employment regulations regarding foreign nationals so once again it would be prudent to make enquiries from the embassies before writing for positions in the country itself.

Beauty in South Africa

The profession of beauty therapy is very well advanced in South Africa which has plenty of beauty therapy colleges as well as salons. Their training syllabus is as comprehensive as those in Britain which means that there is no shortage of their own fully qualified staff. Regrettably their colleges are restricted by the government so there are not many opportunities for other races to train as yet. Once again, the tropical heat of some of South Africa makes the skin very dry so all types of skin treatment programmes are enthusiastically received. It is an extremely sophisticated country with some areas of the population being very wealthy. To find out more about working opportunities there you should write to South Africa House in London.

Beauty around the World

From this it is apparent then that the profession of beauty therapy exists right around the world. The standards are not always the same, but it would be foolish to presume that it is only in Britain that a high standard of beauty education and treatment exists. If you wish to work in another country the best advice could be to write not only to the embassy of that country here in Britain but also to contact the professional beauty therapy organisations of that country for their advice.

4 Treatment planning

Treatment planning

The success or failure of all the beauty treatments offered to clients depends very much on the way in which the therapist approaches the problem, the way in which she assesses the client and the expectations she sets for herself and the client.

In all professional dealings with the public the therapist must be ruthlessly and conscientiously honest. It does not benefit the client or the salon if the client is misled into thinking that the therapist and the treatment are wonder workers.

Regardless of whether the client comes to the salon with a preconceived idea, gained from talking with others or reading about the treatment, she must still have the treatment explained carefully to her. The client of today is not a gullible, mindless idiot. She is quite capable of absorbing information if it is properly explained to her.

This information should cover the type of treatment, why it is necessary, the length of treatment time, the cost and how the client can expect to look or feel afterwards.

If this is done as a routine matter of course, and every new therapist joining the team is instructed to do the same, a lot of explaining as to why instant miracles are not happening, will be avoided.

Body treatments

Grossly obese
Ideally, when dealing with the grossly obese or just obese client, the therapist needs quite a long appointment for the initial

figure consultation as there are so many things to be taken into consideration. However, this is not always possible, particularly in a busy establishment where figure consultations are normally complimentary. Often there is not enough time to carry out a complicated and detailed analysis, so most therapists have to assess all the possibilities and prescribe a course of treatment in a very short space of time. The following is a list of points which should be considered during the first figure analysis:

1 Posture

If the client is grossly obese or even just obese the posture will be greatly affected by the fat deposits so the posture assessment, as taught during training, will not be possible. Heavy fat deposits on inner thigh and knee areas will prevent the client from standing correctly. The weight of an enormous breast will cause a serious rounding of the shoulders and even the straightness of the back will be distorted by rolls of fat. Therefore in cases of gross obesity the posture will have little relevance, although it should be pointed out to the client that her obesity is causing a distortion of her posture.

2 Weight

Although it will be painfully obvious that the client is overweight, it is necessary to weigh her and record that weight. It should also be compared with a reliable height/weight chart and the client should be given a realistic target at which she can aim.

Realistic possibilities

When suggesting a target weight the therapist must ascertain for how long the client has been so overweight. Are there any medical reasons for this? Are there any contra-indications to either weight loss or treatment. It is imperative if the client has more than 6.5 kg (one stone) to lose, that she should be advised to seek permission from her doctor before she embarks on any form of dieting or dietary control. If she has dieted constantly and thereby lowered her metabolic rate it may be necessary to suggest that her doctor be approached for help with this problem.

3 Client co-operation

A rough guide to how much client co-operation one can expect can be gained fom the client herself. Did she enter the room in a confident way? (Shows determination.) Does she speak in a self derogatory manner? (Shows a poor opinion of herself.) Does she make excuses for her present condition? (Most likely to go on blaming external influences.) Does she appear to be able to afford a course or several courses of treatment? (This may appear a very mean and grasping type of question but it will affect the outcome of the treatment. This is why it is always so necessary to be totally honest with clients about length and cost of the course of treatment).

4 Dietary advice

Clients love having a diet sheet thrust at them listing exactly how much of which type of food they may eat, and when. This plan of action is doomed to failure right from the start. The client's taste in foods, her lifestyle, such as how she eats and when she eats, will all affect the outcome. Certainly have some dietary advice sheets printed but they should explain to the client that her present state was caused by eating too much of the wrong type of food in the wrong combinations. A correct eating plan should also be included but it should be as flexible as possible to take in every facet of individual tastes. This is where a calorie count plan is feasible or the weight watchers type of scheme, where foods are exchanged. Advice should also be given regarding items of food that most people suppose to be non-calorific or even 'slimming' such as milk, fruit juice and fruit. These items are sometimes not even listed by the client in her resumé of her daily calorific intake as she presumes them to be free from calories. Again, try to encourage the client to view her weight in the long term strategy and not to expect 'seven-day miracles'.

5 Movement and exercise

Always in conjunction with dietary advice should go the information to the client that it is equally as important to step up her energy output by exercise. The word exercise to some people conjures up visions of hours in a gymnasium or

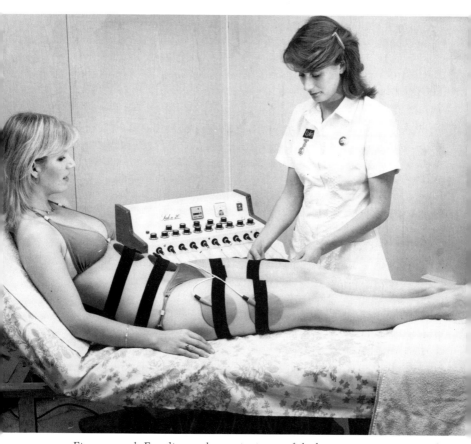

Figure control. Faradic muscle exercise is one of the best treatments to tone and firm the muscles and help prevent cellulite. Coloured pads and a safety start and stop facility make this machine very easy and safe to use

sweating after a heavy aerobic session. If the idea of expending physical energy upsets the client then the therapist must consider other types of exercise such as yoga or isometrics. Even simply walking instead of riding in the car or going swimming should be advised, if it is apparent that the client takes no physical exercise whatsoever. If a gymnasium is available and the client is prepared to follow an exercise routine, great care must be taken to tailor the routine to suit the client's ability and her age.

A combination of diet and exercise which stimulates the

body to eliminate its waste products efficiently and also help rid the body of toxins should be considered a necessity.

6 Treatments available

The type of electrical equipment chosen will depend mainly on the therapist's examination of the body fat itself. Where the fat is hard packed or dimpled and pocketted with fluid (cellulite) then some form of tapotement or pettrisage will be required to break it down and help convert it to soft fat so that it will be more readily assimilated when the body begins to utilise its fat stores. This can take the form of:

(a) *Hand massage.* Very tiring for the therapist who may not be able to exert enough kilos per square centimetre pressure.

(b) *Vacuum massage.* Firstly static cupping followed by the gliding method. If a pulsating machine is available then pulsating followed by gliding.

(c) *Heavy duty electrical vibrator* such as the G5. Effleurage head first, then deeper kneading heads. This machine is quite effective when combined with the vacuum massage machine, particularly on large areas. The G5 machine is used until an erythema is visible and then followed by the vacuum massager used in a lymphatic draining pattern, ie working towards the lymphatic nodes.

(d) *Body galvanic machine.* This is the application of fluids and gels for penetration of the skin by the *iontophoresis method.* The diuretic effect these gels have helps release the trapped body fluids causing a smoothing out of the typical dimpled appearance. This will only be feasible where the fat deposits are localised and are largely the result of poor circulation. Any medical reasons should be referred to the client's doctor. This is also a machine which works well when used in conjunction with the vacuum machine for lymphatic drainage.

(e) *Heating.* The effectiveness of all the machines can be maximised by the use of some form of heating before treatment. Either sauna or steam bath is suitable for these purposes. The ultra violet light beds or lamps should not be used as the erythema already present after irridiation would present problems. The use of the faradic machine should not be

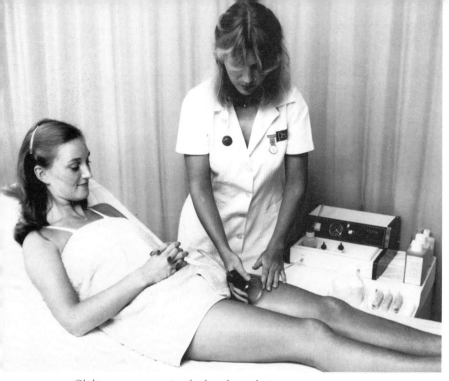

Gliding vacuum suction for lymphatic drainage

A galvanic unit which contains body treatment facilities as well as the facial one

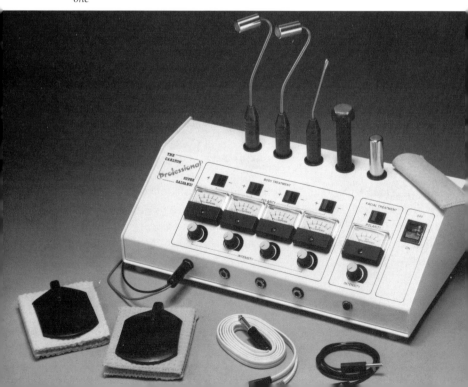

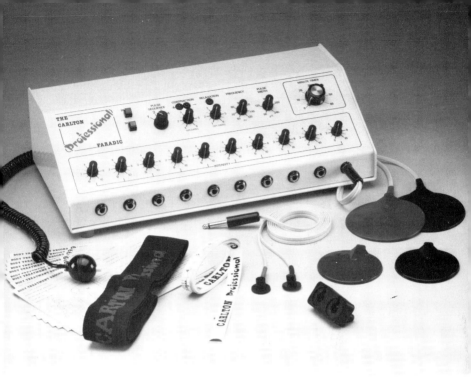

The traditional faradic machine presented with modern styling. This particular machine incorporates a facial electrode as well as the body outlets

A combined galvanic/high frequency unit with easy to see and use controls

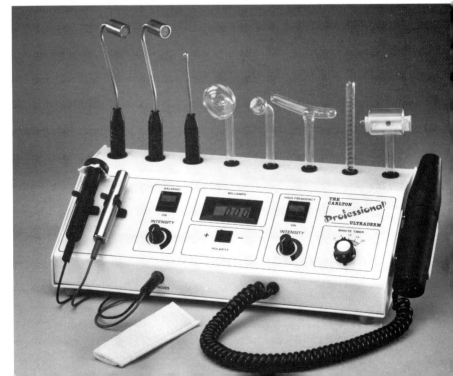

considered in cases of gross obesity as the muscles have great difficulty in functioning properly in areas where they are congested by hard packed fat deposits.

The foregoing are not the only alternatives to treating this type of problem, they are just a brief resumé of the more common methods to be found in the average salon or figure clinic. Many companies promote products designed to help, such as parafango wax, volcanic mud derivatives, as well as herbal remedies. Some are to be used alone, some with heat, and many are designed to be used in conjunction with galvanic current.

Assessing the less overweight

In many figure consultations the acute problems of obesity are not present. Some clients are only marginally overweight, possibly under 6.5 kg (one stone), so in these instances such drastic measures are not needed. Many will have localised fat deposits over abdomen, thighs and buttocks, with sometimes middle and upper back involvement. In these instances the scheme of work should be as follows:

1 A recommended weight loss.

2 Improved metabolic rate due to stimulation from exercising.

3 After testing for muscle tone, faradic muscle toning with or without vacuum massage for lymphatic drainage.

4 G5 massage to improve circulation.

Contra-indications

All the foregoing information pre-supposes that the client has been checked for contra-indications. At no time should the therapist ever consider giving a treatment where there is the slightest suspicion that the client may be contra-indicated. Even if the client insists that it doesn't matter and that she is prepared to take full responsibility, it is against the Code of Ethics of the profession to ignore any contra-indications.

Body massage

Not everyone who comes to the body room is necessarily overweight. Very often clients without a weight problem or even underweight ones will consult the therapist for treatment. This is usually for body massage, and often for vague aches and pains due to tension. These must all be checked to see if there is a medical problem present and great care must be taken to ensure that they are not at present receiving treatment from either their doctor or another practitioner for this problem.

When body massage is decided upon the client should have some form of pre-heating first, such as steam bath or sauna. The massage couch should be in the quietest, most private part of the salon and the therapist must leave instructions with all other staff, particularly reception, that she is not to be disturbed during this treatment period.

After careful consultation any one of the following treatments could be performed provided that the therapist has had the proper training for it.

1 **A stimulating massage** to counteract a tendency to sluggishness. This could be done with either a G5 vibrator or a very strong manual massage which includes mainly pettrisage and tapotement movements.

2 **A relaxation massage** with plenty of effluerage and relaxatory movements. This could also include the use of an audio-sonic vibrator over certain these areas, particularly over tension nodules which are mostly found in the upper fibres of the trapezius, near the aponeurosis.

3 **Aromatherapy massage.** This is not just an ordinary body massage using aromatic oils. Obviously it bears a great similarity to Swedish massage but it is a technique designed for the maximum absorption of the remedial properties of the oils both through the skin and through the olifactory system.

4 **Shiatsu.** This form of massage is often described as acupressure. It is a method of relieving stress and related aches and pains and other minor ailments through varying degrees of pressure on certain pressure points. These pressure points are closely related to the acupuncture points and meridians.

Reflexology

This is a method of helping clients with minor health problems through massaging certain points on the feet.

It cannot be stressed enough, however, that the above mentioned techniques should not be attempted by anyone who has not had adequate training and passed an examination in them. Addresses of training establishment for these ancillary subjects can be found in the appendix of this book.

Running the figure clinic

Managing a successful figure clinic requires a great dedication and also a patient and persevering temperament. Clients are attracted initially to the clinic in an attempt to have their problems sorted out by someone else, but it is obvious that they must be made aware that the onus is on them to persevere and succeed. There are no magic 'bacon slicing' machines available, but all the therapist does have can help if used sensibly and realistically.

The figure clinic will attract a lot of clients and keep them, only if it is scrupulously clean and with good principles of hygiene. Hygiene is like justice, not only must it be done but also it must be seen to be done. For instance, all client dressing gowns should be removed and placed in the dirty laundry bin as soon as the client has left the cubicle. Never hang up a gown where someone might accidentally give it to another client. When clean gowns are brought back into the salon after washing they should be placed in plastic bags and put in one special place so that there can be no confusion between clean and dirty ones. When offering the clean one, let the client see you remove it from the plastic bag.

A steam bath should be cleaned thoroughly as soon as the client has left it so that germs cannot multiply in the warm moist atmosphere. A disposable towel should be placed on the seat of the steam bath before each client sits in it. There should also be a disposable towel placed on the floor where the client will put her feet. The sponge covers for the active and indifferent electrode of the galvanic machine should be washed

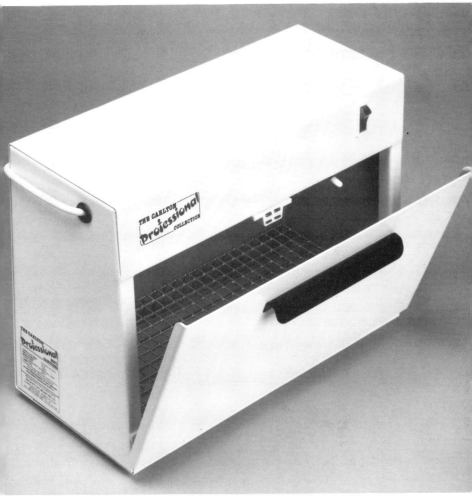

Sterilising cabinet for all small equipment and brushes. These use ultra violet light for sterilising so brushes should not be wrapped in tissue before being placed in the cabinet as the light cannot strike the important surfaces

thoroughly in warm water as soon as they are taken off the client's skin as the salts from the gels and the skins surface will discolour them. Once discoloured they should be replaced by new ones.

Faradic machine pads should be washed in an antiseptic solution between each client. The body straps of these machines can look an awful mess if they are not kept in some orderly fashion. They should either be patiently rewound after use by each client or hung over a convenient rail and the ends fitted together. Nothing looks worse than an untidy jumble of body straps in a cubicle.

Beds and couches should first be covered with a blanket and then with a full cover of disposable paper. This should, of course, be changed between each client. All trolley and unit tops should be neat and tidy with bottles and jars neatly labelled. Wooden spatulas should be available for removal of cream from jars. Germs are spread if fingers are dipped in cream jars.

The figure clinic should be light and airy but warm with plenty of magazines and places for clients to put their clothes. The one golden rule should be that there is a member of staff present in the figure clinic at all times and no client should be left wired up to either a galvanic or a faradic machine without a member of staff supervising her and being constantly within sight and sound.

Safety at all times should be the motto of every figure clinic. All machines must be checked not only by the therapist every time she uses it but also regularly by an electrician familiar with this type of machinery.

Safety in the sun-bed room

The sun-bed area or room needs a very strict observance to the rules of safety and hygiene. All beds should be cleansed by a member of staff after each client, using disposable paper towelling and a disinfectant solution formulated specially for sun-beds. This cleaning should also include the pillow if one is present but it is often more hygienic to suggest that the client brings her own towel to use rolled up under her head. A container of antiseptic solution should be near to the bed so that the goggles can be left soaking between each use. Once a week it will be necessary to remove the acrylic sheet surface and clean underneath it. Paper towels should be readily available in the area for the client to use.

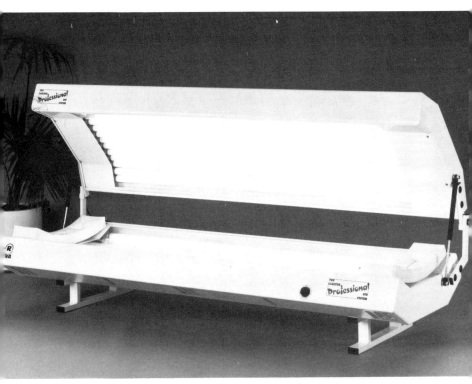

Sun-beds come in all shapes and sizes but this one demonstrates good design combined with professional facilities

Clients should not be allowed to use the sun-beds unless they have been checked for contra-indications and they have signed their record card in agreement that these procedures have been carried out. Every client should be asked if she is familiar with this type of sun-bed and, if not, a member of staff must demonstrate to the client the safe use of the beds. Clients should never be allowed more than the recommended times for irradiation and should be monitored carefully. Clients should never be allowed to take children with them into the sun-bed area for the children to sit and wait for the parents. Where this has been allowed to happen, the mother has been seen lying on the bed wearing protective goggles and the child has been standing staring at the light with no protection over the eyes whatsoever!

The running hours of each bed should be carefully logged in a book specially for the purpose. When the recommended burning hours of the tubes has been reached they should be changed whether they are still lighting or not. Tubes exhaust their tanning abilities after their recommended time and it is of no financial benefit to leave them in a bed because they are still lighting. If the client is not tanning then the salon will get a lot of complaints or worse, the client will go elsewhere.

Shower facilities
Shower facilities are an absolute must if one plans to have even one sun-bed on the premises. Clients must be instructed to remove all deodorants, perfumes and creams from the skin and lie on the bed with a scrupulously clean skin for maximum benefit and safety reasons. This would not be possible if the salon did not offer a free shower facility.

Although many clients are quite happy to use most of the facilities on a communal basis, the sun-beds are a different proposition. Most clients prefer to tan without any clothing which makes it absolutely imperative to have privacy for the sun-beds. Either curtained cubicles or cubicles of louvred screens are suitable.

In all figure clinics and treatment rooms where clients are changing and leaving their clothes and belongings, one should make every effort to arrange lockable facilities. If this is not possible then notices disclaiming any responsibility must be prominently displayed and clients should be discouraged from wearing or bringing anything of great value when they attend for treatment.

Keeping records

It is imperative that a very strict and comprehensive system of keeping a record of every client be devised. All sections of the card should be filled in, particularly an address and telephone number. In instances of staff illness it is so essential to be able to contact the client. It is also useful when a special promotion is being arranged if a complete mailing list of all clients, preferably divided into body, sun-bed, or face and electrolysis treatments, can be to hand.

Any previous medical history of operations, etc, and any contra-indication present should always be listed so that new members of staff should be able to take over a client and be immediately in the picture. With sun-bed record cards, the client should always be asked to sign the card to say that she has been asked about contra-indications and also that she has been instructed in the use of the beds.

Every time a client attends for treatment it should be noted on the card together with details of treatment received. If a course of treatment is being payed for at one time, then marks should be noted on the card listing how many treatments have been bought and some method devised of marking these off every time the client attends so that there is no argument as to how many of her sessions she has received.

The face clinic

In smaller establishments the figure clinic and the facial unit will probably be one and the same, but where space permits, it is useful to have a separate space devoted exclusively to facial treatments. In this area it is much more comfortable for the client to lie in the padded reclining adjustable chairs rather than on a couch. If finances are limited then a couch with an adjustable head can be utilised, but the chairs are more adaptable both for client and for the height of the individual therapist. The therapist must always be aware of her own posture and realise that working at the wrong height or at an uncomfortable angle can cause severe back problems for herself.

An adjustable operator's stool is also a good idea so that the therapist can either stand or sit, depending on her own preferences. These should be well padded and preferably on wheels so that there is a great freedom of movement.

Adequate lighting is another essential element in this section. If fluorescent lighting is installed, try experimenting with different types of tubes. Some are harsh daylight while

CUSTOMER RECORD CARD

Name:.. Age:................................ Tel. No.:................

Address: ....

PERSONAL DOCTOR	DETAILS OF PRESCRIBED DRUGS
Name:	
Address:	
Telephone No.:	

MEDICAL HISTORY

Height: Weight: Chest: Waist: Hips:

Heart Disease: Yes/No   Varicose Veins: Yes/No

Details of Operations:_____

_____

_____

Other Comments: _____

_____

Date	Treatment	Remarks

others have a softer effect. Avoid the ones with a strong yellow tinge to them as this makes any skin look very yellow. An independent source of light from a cold light magnifier is essential both for skin analysis and for electrolysis if this area is also to be used for this treatment.

Trolley and unit tops should be kept as free from clutter as possible, with only the very basic necessary jars and bottles on display. Adequate storage both of cupboards and drawer space should be readily to hand with all necessary materials and tools neatly arranged for the therapist to use with the minimum amount of disturbance to the client. Some larger salons prefer to have everything kept in a separate room such as a kitchen/dispensary and to have the trolleys laid up there with everything being prepared, often by a junior member of staff, before the treatment commences with the client being shown into an empty cubicle and the trolley brought in after her. The amount of space available usually governs the layout of most establishments.

Most of the equipment manufacturers are displaying the stacking type of units, where all the necessary facial machines such as high frequency, faradic, galvanic, electrolysis, steam and desquamating brushes are all neatly housed in one stacking unit. These are often expensive but where space is more limited they are an ideal purchase.

Soft cellular blankets in colours which blend with the general colour scheme, together with toning towels and matching headbands, complete the requirements of each cubicle or room. Once again, hygiene is so important and the client will notice very quickly if anything looks used or grubby. Blankets which contain a mixture of wool and man-made fibres are obviously the best choice so that they can go through the salon's washing machine rather than requiring constantly to to dry cleaned. Many of the beds and couches, which have been designed specifically for the beauty salon, incorporate a facility for the disposable paper towel roll to be fixed to it. This can then be laid over the top of blankets in order to avoid soiling and to create an impression of pristine freshness.

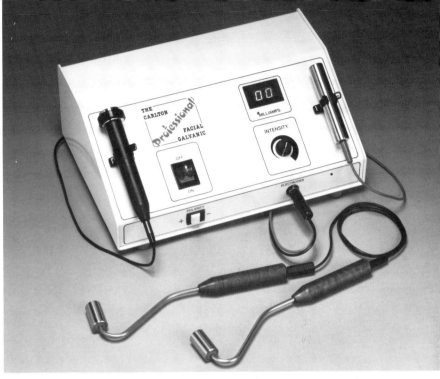

Single galvanic facial unit which fits neatly in with other equipment or can be used individually. A compact size for the visiting beauty therapist

A modern clinical epilation unit which has facilities for either footswitch or hand operation by button on needle holder

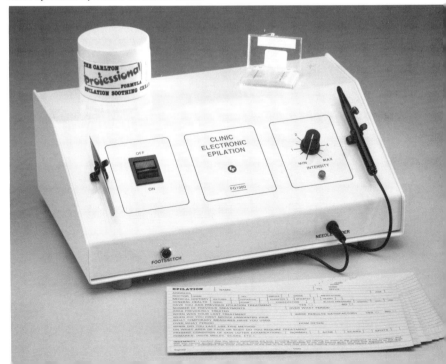

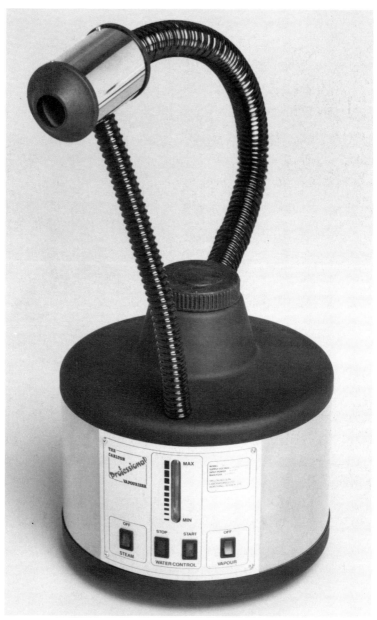

Table or trolley standing face steamer with a variable direction arm which enables the flow of steam to be directed at different angles to suit the individual client

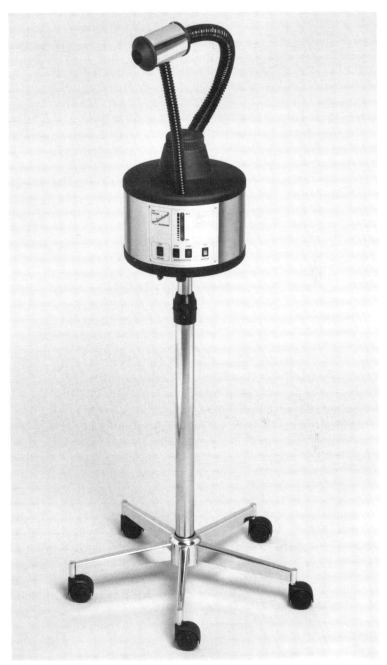

Floor standing version of the multi-directional steamer. The five-footed stand maximises the stability of this unit

Facial analysis

At the completion of training the new beauty therapist usually feels that the world is peopled with problem skins. So much has been taught about severe skin conditions that one imagines every client that comes in will have some severe condition or other. In the majority of salons this is not so. Most of the skins basically have one thing wrong with them and that is neglect! Probably not wilful neglect, but neglect all the same, often through ignorance. Those that do follow a daily cleansing routine will often be using products which are either wrong or inadequate for their type of skin. Despite all that has been written over the past decade in women's magazines and beauty books about cleansing the skin according to its type, one still sees a tremendous amount of dry skins being scrubed with soap and flannel!

During the first consultation with the client, the therapist must firstly examine the skin through the magnifier, and then question the client closely about her present skin routine. Again the outcome of any plan of treatment must be explained carefully to the client so that she is aware of the present condition of her skin, the types of treatment which can be used to help, and what she can expect at the completion of treatment. Extravagant claims for specific treatments or products should never be made. The client should always be given a realistic forecast and should also be made aware that in most cases the old cliche 'prevention is better than cure', really is true.

This is very much the case with mature and wrinkling skin where so many external forces affect the degree of ageing present. Many clients are not aware that their lifestyle and diet affect the condition of the skin tremendously. Smoking, spending most of the day in centrally heated or air conditioned premises, walking through traffic and inhaling carbon monoxide and lead pollutants all have an adverse effect on the body's ability to regenerate its cellular structure. It is also fashionable at the moment to blame food additives for everything, but it has been proven by research that they, as well as the toxins which we consume in foods such as coffee and tea, can have an adverse effect on human skin.

It is the duty of the beauty therapist to be as well read as she can possibly be on the subject of the human body and the way it works. Not only from anatomy and physiology books, which are the bain of the student therapist's life, but also on all types of writing on subjects which affect our lifestyles. A list of recommended reading is included in the appendix and the therapist should always read up on every new theory. This does not mean that everything read should be believed, but the caring therapist should be aware of all the theories presented and use her own trained skill in deciding which she thinks most credible. It should be remembered that many clients are extremely knowledgeable and it is the duty of every therapist to know at least as much as the clients, and preferably to know much more. The remainder of the clients do no reading at all and are in total ignorance so it is also the duty of the therapist to try to enlighten them about the things which are affecting their health and appearance.

Vitamin therapy is another facet of health on which the therapist should be very knowledgeable. Many clients are interested in vitamins and a plan of healthy eating but often lack the chance to obtain unbiased information on the subject.

Diagnosing skin types

The correct diagnosis of the skin type is so vitally important that great care should be taken over it. It should be remembered, however, that it is only a guide and often a client can have a skin type which changes with the seasons. Regardless of what the skin was at the last visit, the plan of treatment must take into account the condition of the skin at the time of treatment. Often just one treatment will make a considerable difference, so a planned course of treatment may need minor changes made to it.

With a sensitive skin it must be remembered that it can be present with any of the other conditions, either normal, dry, greasy, or a combination. Another common mistake in skin diagnosis is presuming that if open pores are present they are the sign of a greasy or, at least, a combination skin. Open pores can often be found on a mature either normal or dry skin and are due to the ageing process occurring in the superficial layers of the epidermis.

Planning a treatment programme

If a client is in the clinic for her very first facial it is a good idea to do only a basic routine. Regardless of the skin diagnosis, it is best to get her complete confidence and relax her by doing only a basic deep cleanse, facial massage, masque, cleanse and tone without the use of any electrical equipment at all.

It should be explained to her that a more complicated facial routine which involves the use of electrical equipment would suit her and that you propose to do that at her next visit. This at least gives her the chance to say that she would prefer not to have the treatment or agree to it, particularly as the more involved facials are usually priced higher.

When a client has not had a facial treatment before she may be very apprehensive and concerned thinking that it may hurt or even alter her in some way. Once she has become accustomed to you and your hands being on her in a relaxing manner, her fears will be dispelled. As therapists we are used to handling people physically with our hands, but many clients are not in the habit of any physical contact and are sometimes scared by it.

Choice of facial routine

A sensible therapist is one who tries to give as wide and varied a range of treatments as possible. One school of thought suggests that all the good therapist needs is a well-trained pair of hands and a jar of cream. This is a good basis to begin with, but clients are much more selective and enlightened about the treatments and equipment available and even in the smallest salon one can be asked for the most sophisticated facials. the following are just a few suggested combinations:

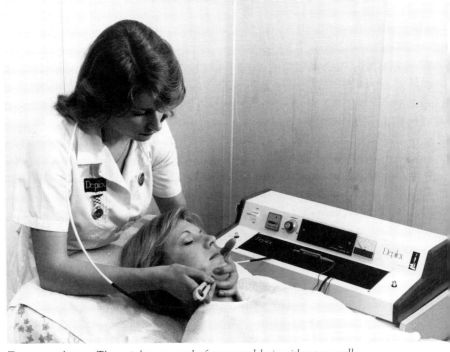

Tweezer epilation. The painless removal of unwanted hair without a needle

Air massage. Gentle and effective facial massage without stretching the skin

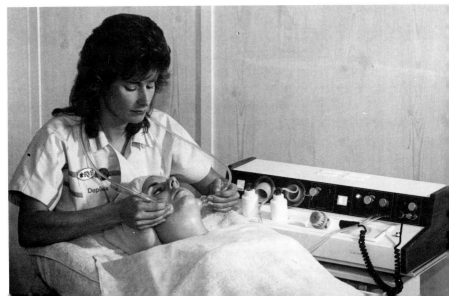

Cleansing: by brush, biological skin peel, desincrustation using galvanic current, or by vacuum suction.

Massage: by hand, audio-sonic vibrators, percussion vibrators. Lymphatic drainage massage of face and neck area by vacuum massage.

Treatment: galvanic desincrustation, galvanic iontophoresis, high frequency both direct and indirect, faradic stimulation of muscles, laser therapy, and many others.

Masques: desquamating, stimulating, cleansing and refining, hydrating, cooling and de-sensitising clays, gels, creams, colloidals. Oil combined with heat application. Paraffin wax.

Creams, liquids and ampoules: Oil in water emulsions, water in oil suspensions, humectants, collagen, placenta extracts, aloe vera, balsam, primrose oil, aromatherapy oils, royal jelly, and many other plant or herbal productions.

Every competent therapist should be able to put together a wide range of facial treatments using a permutation of any of the equipment together with the products listed, as well as the hundreds available and not listed. Care should be taken, however, not to get too gimmicky with facials. Most therapists tend to settle for about ten or twelve variations on the theme, ones which they know from experience give good results.

Laser therapy

There have been such bad press reports regarding the use of this treatment that, quite naturally, there is anxiety about its use in beauty therapy. The name *Laser* is an abbreviation of the initials of Light Amplification by Stimulated Emission of Radiation. There are many types of lasers in use but the most dramatic appears to be the medical application of the CO_2 laser which has a cutting and cauterising effect on the skin, and the argon laser which causes immediate coagulation. When used by a highly skilled and qualified surgeon they can be invaluable in treating all sorts of medical problems involving the skin. Most spectacular results have been achieved when treating such disfiguring marks as port-wine stain birthmarks.

The application of lasers in beauty therapy has been brought into disrepute by unscrupulous operators attempting to use the CO_2 lasers and others for retarding the ageing process and other skin treatments, but causing untold damage instead. This unfortunately has overshadowed the good research that has been going on by respected members of the profession and commercial companies attempting to produce a safe method.

The type of laser most favoured by the British companies appears to be the low powered helium neon laser. Research carried out by a reputable company reports that there was a noticeable reduction in the small fine wrinkles on the panel of subjects who allowed themselves to be used for the tests. It has been suggested that once a course of treatment has been started with the laser, it should be followed up by regular repeats of

Brush cleansing unit for desincrustation and deep cleansing

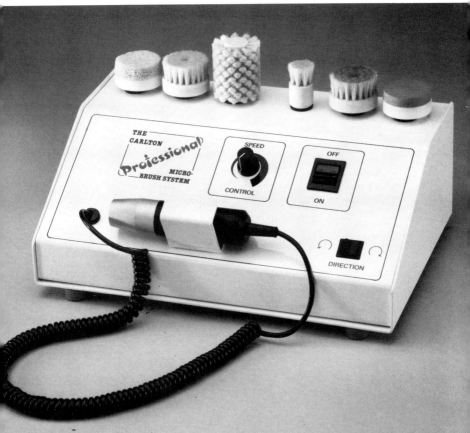

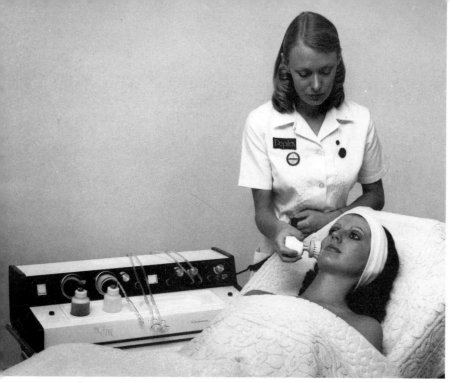

Cosmetic brushing

Galvanic facial with roller electrodes

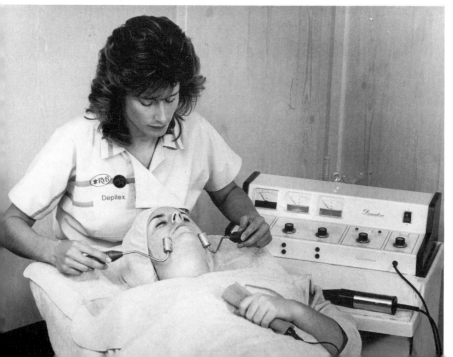

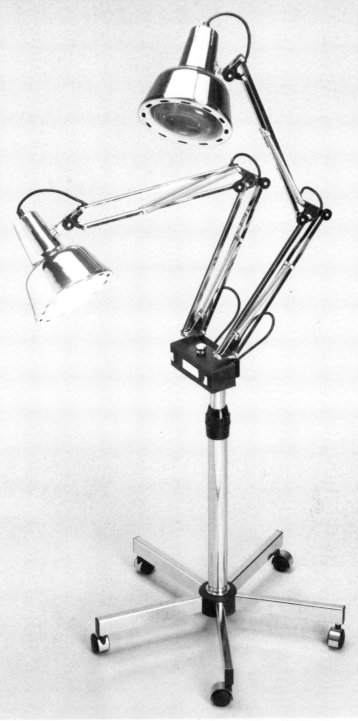

Multi-armed light which can give normal light or infra red/radiant heat therapy

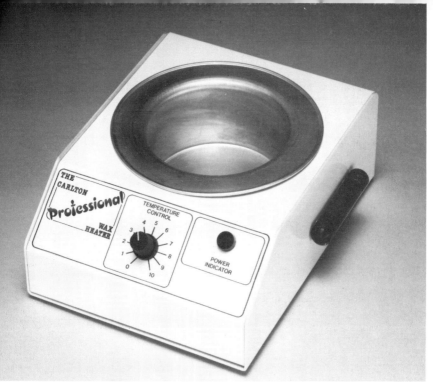

A stream-lined style soft wax heater with stainless steel basin which makes cleaning so easy

A double wax heater with a built in automatic filtering device. This is essential when working with the traditional hot wax

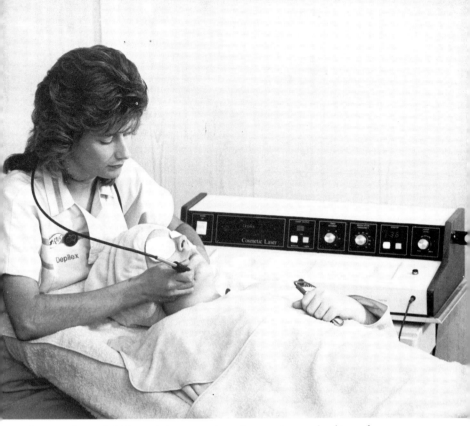

Cosmetic laser. Cold beam helium neon laser firms and tones the skin and improves healing

treatment. These machines, as with all the others mentioned, can usually be seen at beauty exhibitions and conferences all around the country. As with all new equipment, it is up to the individual therapist to use her own judgement in deciding whether she would be happy using the machine and if she could produce results to the benefit of her clients.

Electrolysis

As controversial a subject as lasers, when it was first introduced as a treatment for the removal of unwanted hair earlier this century, electrolysis has become one of the most popular treatments any beauty establishment can offer. Proficiency at the skill of electrolysis is, however, a very difficult art to acquire. The student electrologist requires hours of patient practise before she is capable of probing a follicle accurately. It was originally performed by using a machine operating on the galvanic principle but in latter years that has been superceded in popularity by the more widely used short wave diathermy method. Some operators use a technique blending both galvanic and short wave diathermy methods called, appropriately enough, 'the blend'. This would appear to be more popular in the USA and some continental countries than in the UK.

While the majority of clients attending for electrolysis are troubled by hair on the face and neck, there is now a growing demand for electrolysis of the legs and bikini line area.

The complexity of the problem and the length of treatment should all be explained to a client before she undertakes a course of treatment. It is customary in most salons to invite clients to have a complimentary consultation when the therapist can explain the treatment fully. This can be done with the help of diagrams and wall charts, originally designed for teaching electrolysis, so the client can understand exactly what is happening to her. Her fears about scarring can be allayed at that initial consultation and if possible a few hairs should be probed so that the client can feel what degree of discomfort is entailed.

It is in the field of electrolysis that the therapist's most vigilant care must be taken with hygiene. Every therapist should now be using either disposable needles which are thrown away after every treatment or the very high temperature sterilisers designed for such a purpose. Care must also be taken when disposing of used needles. They should always be disposed of in a special 'sharps' box which is then handed to the local refuse disposal team. Needles should never be disposed of in the ordinary waste or litter system.

Ancillary treatments

There are many other ancillary treatments which make up the list of services offered by most salons. Some of them highly

An electrolysis needle steriliser which heats the inner granules to extremely high temperatures thereby effectively killing all possible germs. This is very necessary if pre-sterilised needles are not available

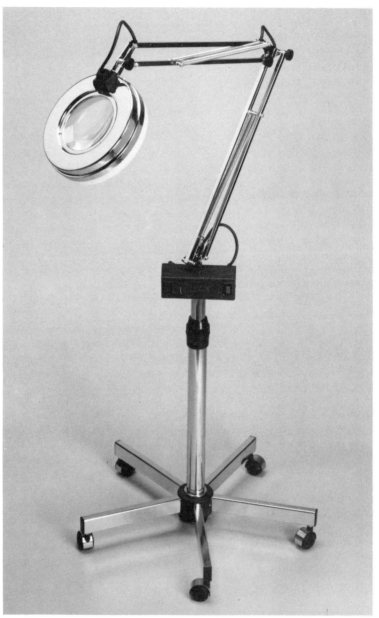

The stainless steel cold light magnifying screen which is essential in an electrolysis clinic for accurate probing

profitable like leg waxing, and some of them unprofitable, and only offered as a form of service to encourage clients into the salon, such as manicures and pedicures.

Although many of the newer nail extension systems are in great demand and appear to be fool-proof, they are not quite the money spinner that the suppliers would have you believe. Once fitted with these nails some of the clients appear to do the most amazing things, which always results in them becoming damaged and needing replacing. One could write a book alone on the excuses one hears for broken false nails. Whilst they do indeed attract clients to the salon, be prepared to have a lot of problems with them and a much lower profit ratio than appears apparent at first.

However, the wise salon owner makes her treatment list as comprehensive as possible so that there is no possible need for a client to go elsewhere for treatment.

Promoting treatments

To make the clients aware of all the services you offer and to attract new custom, the therapist must always be looking at new ways of promoting business. Attractive and imaginative 'in salon' advertising of different treatments certainly helps.

Areas such as in the waiting and reception area and the changing rooms should all have imaginative posters detailing treatments available, as well as on the walls where body treatment couches are situated. There you have a captive audience, eager for something to read. Paper pamphlets or brochures listing the whole range of services should be freely available for clients to take for their friends. These should have the salon name and telephone number boldly displayed on the front.

Dull lists of treatments make boring reading so take a little time and imagination and describe many of the services in detail. Also think of some promotional linking of several treatments together with a view to increasing work. Why not have a 'Summer Special', including all the treatment one usually wants before a summer holiday such as sun-tan, leg wax and pedicure. Lump the three together, take a slight reduction off the cost because the client is having them at the same time and you then have your summer special.

When the traditional autumn lull comes, try advertising an 'Autumn Bonanza' comprising of steam bath, body massage and facial. Perhaps a 'Christmas Cracker' containing a facial, eyelash tint and manicure. The specials do not necessarily need to be seasonal things. Why not advertise something like 'Beautiful Eyes' consisting of eyebrow shape, eyelash tint, a gentle massage around the delicate eye area with a special eye gel, perhaps followed by a very light application of galvanic iontophoresis over the fine crows feet and wrinkles around the outer eye area, finished off with a rest of 10 to 15 minutes with eyepads soaked in eye toner. The idea should be imaginative but not gimmicky.

If there is something like a local marathon race or walk going on, let your windows or advertising feature a 'Happy Feet' special. A pedicure with lots of extras would fit this occasion. Try to offer a voucher for treatment as a prize in any kind of competition your local newspaper is running. Anything to keep your name or the name of the salon before the potential clients.

Retail selling

Many therapists hate the idea of retail selling, but it does not need to be the hard sell. Nothing is worse for loosing clients than the thought that they can't get out of the salon unless they buy something from an over-enthusiastic therapist. It does make sense, however, to back up that extensive range of salon treatments with a complementary range of retail lines.

It is a good idea to take your time deciding which line to stock as it should be a range which the client cannot obtain elsewhere in your area. Some cosmetic houses will restrict their sales to salons only but these are few and far between. Usually they tend to be in the higher price range although most clients expect creams and cosmetics purchased in the salon to be much more expensive than they often are.

Whatever line you choose, it should be one in which you have complete confidence so that you can suggest it with a clear conscience and always offer a money back guarantee if the client is not completely satisfied.

Dealing with complaints
A problem frequently encountered by the new therapist is what does one do about complaints. Don't despair, even the best therapist encounters a few complaints from time to time, either about a retail product or even sometimes about a treatment.

The first thing is not immediately to presume that the client is right and you must be at fault. At least 50% of your complaints will come from people who could almost be described as professional complainers. Never, never allow a client to sound off with a load of complaints at the top of her voice in front of other clients! Quietly and politely make an offer to see her by appointment to listen to her grievances. Be as honest and just as you can. If you feel she has even a small reason for complaint then do remedy it by offering either another treatment or her money back. If, however, you can honestly believe that there are no grounds for complaint then you must be firm and say so. This is why it is so important to be scrupulously honest when suggesting a line of treatment or a retail purchase, so that there are no misconceptions in the client's mind as to what the end result will be.

Safety in the salon

A final point to raise is the question of safety. Always think **safety first**. It may sound childish and silly but never leave room for any complaints over safety. If there is a loose piece of carpet you may be sure someone will fall over it, and present you with a bill for a fracture of the wrist or worse! It is imperative that one member of the staff, if not all of them, has attended first aid classes and all are made very aware of safety routines and fire drills. All these things may seem unnecessary but, like insurance, you are glad you have them if ever the need arises!

5 A salon of your own

The urge to be one's own boss burns fiercely in most members of the beauty profession. Indeed the majority of beauty establishments are owner operated, sometimes solely on their own but often with assistants as well. The larger establishments that are owned by a non-qualified person are very much in the minority, although the number is now increasing due to the popularity of a beauty room being an added attraction on a variety of commercial ventures such as hotels, health clubs, dance studios and even golf clubs.

A working plan

Self-employment is not a thing to be entered into lightly as there are many snags which are not envisaged in the first flush of enthusiasm. Each person's case, however, would differ so it would be up to the individual therapist to consider the whole idea very seriously and weigh up both the advantages and disadvantages in order to decide if she really could make a success of such a venture.

An ideal way to start is to get pen and paper together and write down a complete plan of the proposed venture. Lay out all the expenses first, showing setting up costs separately from the recurring weekly and monthly expenses. Then work out the number of hours proposed as a working day. If you intend to work from 9 until 5 with an hour off for lunch then you will be working a 7 hour day. Multiply this by how many days you intend working in the week. Say for instance 5 days. This would then give the figure of $5 \times 7 = 35$ hours per week worked.

The next step would be to list all the expenses that would occur. Starting with the most obvious large figures such as rent, rates, lighting, heating, telephone and not forgetting the amount of money which has to be paid into the bank each week to repay a loan, if it was necessary to incur one, to cover set up costs. Another large sum which is often overlooked is that of the cost of materials for use. Treatment creams, cosmetics, powders, mask materials, wax, waxing strips, cotton wool, tissues, protective bed rolls, all mount up to quite a sizeable expenditure every week. This particular figure is very difficult to assess as, quite obviously, it will differ according to how much work you are doing. It can also vary considerably depending on the quality of the products you are using. A word of warning, however, cheapest is not necessarily the best in the long run. One must always be aware of the cost of materials and make all treatments as cost effective as possible, but not at the risk of losing clients due to the poor quality of the products used.

Then there are the smaller costs such as insurances, a constant supply of new magazines, coffee and tea, flowers for the reception area, even down to estimating toilet rolls needed. When a final gross figure is arrived at for the proposed working week, divide it by the number of hours one is intending to work to find the basic hourly cost of running the salon. This figure does not include any wage that you intend to pay yourself.

Now calculate how much an average treatment would cost per hour in the proposed salon, bearing in mind, the location of the salon, the type of area it is in, whether there are any other salons in the area and if there are, their current prices. This figure multiplied by the number of hours one intends working (in the example I estimated 45 hours) gives an estimated income per week and should promptly be cut by half! Even in the busiest salon a therapist cannot work every hour, non-stop, of the working week. In a new salon where a clientele does not already exist, one can quite confidently expect to find that on some days one would only have a very few clients. A common mistake made by the enthusiastic beginner is to believe that the whole world is just sitting there waiting for you to open the salon door. Clients have to be wooed and won!

After those very rough estimates the idea is to compare the hourly cost of running the salon with our 'guesstimated' hourly figure that we think the salon will produce as an income per hour figure. Obviously the income per hour figure must be larger than the expenses per hour figure, and larger by quite a substantial amount or there will not be any income at all for the therapist. This may all seem very obvious but it is surprising how many enthusiastic, would be self employed beginners, omit this very crucial step of making a working plan.

Financing the plan

The plan is even more important if one has to raise money to finance the initial costs of setting up the salon. Regardless of where one borrows the money, it is businesslike and expected to present your finance source with a carefully worked out plan of this kind. How can you give the impression that you can run a venture in a businesslike fashion, if you do not have any idea what kind of expenses you are likely to encounter and how you could pay both the expenses and repay the proposed loan?

Borrowing money can be the easiest thing in the world or the most difficult! It depends on how you ask, and from whom? Firstly look at your own finances. You may be wealthier than you thought. If you already own your own home then this can often be used as collateral or security against a loan from a bank.

Perhaps you have a relative, husband, or parents willing to help. This might solve the problem of high interest rates, but it would only be fair when working out the rate at which you intend to repay this loan, to include some of the interest which the money would have been earning if it were invested.

Finance houses are another possible source but they are basically a much more costly method of financing. With most small businesses the most likely person to listen to you is your local branch of one of the big banks. All them have some package deal or other designed especially for such a business venture as this. A telephone call to the manager of your local branch, asking for an appointment to see him is the first step. However, he will probably look more favourably at your request if you already have an account in his bank, though this is not absolutely necessary, and it varies from bank to bank. What he will expect is a carefully prepared plan, as already mentioned, showing exactly how much money you wish to borrow, if you have any security to offer him against this loan, and how you intend repaying it. Another question he will want answered is for how long you wish to borrow the money. All these questions and answers help him decide which form of loan he will be willing to offer you. Of course his main interest is in gaining more customers, who will then use his banking facilities and therefore be charged for this use, and in making more money for his bank in the form of interest that has to be paid on every loan.

Overdraft or loan?

An overdraft is mainly a method of lending/borrowing money which is seldom encountered in any other country outside Great Britain. The bank manager agrees, after discussing your projects and cash requirements, to allow you to spend up to £X number of pounds. You do not have to spend it all at once, you may spend some of it, repay and spend again, but what you may **not** do, is go over the agreed sum. The bank makes its money by charging you a certain percentage over what is called 'base rate'. This is the rate at which the bank gets its money and the percentage over bank or base rate which you will be charged is the bank's profit. This really is an old method of lending money and was really intended very much as a short term measure. You borrowed money from the bank because you knew that your ship would soon be home with a fabulous cargo which, when sold, would make a great deal of money. The bank would then be repaid and everyone would be happy. However, business is not like that these days and most bank managers would prefer you to agree to a set amount loaned, at a set figure of interest, and most importantly with a set time in which the money must be repaid.

These are called 'term loans' and can be for a short or long term. These loans are favoured much more by bank managers, particularly if this is your first loan with their bank, because you and your abilities to run a venture efficiently are very much unknown quantities. Most bank managers are skilled at listening to enthusiastic schemes and sifting through all the information you are presenting to them. Try not to be offended if they suggest that some of your wilder ideas are a bit far fetched. Whatever you may think you are capable of doing, they are equally capable of seeing that some ventures will never really get off the ground, often for simple reasons that you may have overlooked.

Likewise, don't be put off by the first bank manager that refuses to lend you money. He may already be over-committed on his loan area, he may have had someone in the beauty business recently gone bankrupt owing his bank a lot of money, or he may just be in a bad mood today. On the other hand, however, if you have worked out your proposed plan as accurately and honestly as you can, presented yourself in a neat and tidy and businesslike manner and you get turned down by a second bank manager, then think again. Always think of the bank manager as the man who needs to lend money! Therefore, if he doesn't want to lend it to you, you must look again at your plan. Are you being realistic? Do you really think that you will be able to work for the very low figure that you had allotted for yourself? Had you taken into account that at the end of the first year the income tax man is going to require a sizable sum of money from you in tax? If your loan application is turned down by a bank manager, ask him quite politely why, and you may find the answer to your problems. This is, of course, presuming that he is going to say no! If, however, he says yes, then you are in business. What kind of move you make from here depends very much what you had in your plan. Perhaps you intended buying an already existing business?

Buying an existing business

This may appear at first sight to be the simplest way of starting yourself in business, but it may not always be so. Many therapists who had difficulties when first entering business might have got on better had they started from scratch. The first thing you have to decide is why the present owners are selling the business. Please do not believe everything a person selling a business tells you. It is a terrible fact of life, but when people are trying to get themselves out of an unworkable situation they will often tell a whole series of white lies, and a few rather dirty ones as well! Insist on seeing audited accounts on the last few years of trading and don't take no for an answer. The old story about the books being with either the Income Tax inspector or the accountant just will not wash! Insist that you will come back and continue with negotiations only when they telephone to say that the books or statements of accounts are there to be seen. Also make sure they have some stamp of authenticity such as the Income Tax office stamp or that of some reputable firm of accountants. Even then, they may not be a true picture of the current state of the business. Keep your eyes open and look around you. Has another salon opened recently in the area. Are they bigger?, better? or just more efficient and pleasant than the owner of the business you are contemplating buying?

A prospective buyer of an hotel once asked to see the recent laundry bills rather than the 'books'. When asked why, she replied that in the hotel industry the cost of laundering sheets, towels and table cloths was a very expensive item so it was very unlikely that anyone would launder sheets that had not been slept in. The laundry bills, therefore, represented to her a truer guide to how many guests had been staying at the hotel than the actual 'books'!

Make sure you know exactly what is being offered for sale. Is all the equipment on display in the transaction? Ask to see receipts of when it was purchased to give yourself a true picture of its value. It may have cost £600 six years ago, and the new model may be selling currently for £900 but a six year old machine which has been in constant use and serviced very infrequently is worth only a very small fraction of its original price.

Goodwill is also a very difficult thing to purchase. It is a very elusive commodity which is difficult to assess when agreeing on a figure with the vendors (people who are selling the business). If a salon is called, for example, Betty's Beauty World and has been run exclusively by Betty who is quite a local personality and well known in the area, there is not likely to be much saleable goodwill left in the business once Betty goes, particularly if she opens up a new salon half a mile away despite her repeatedly telling you that she was going to join her sister in Australia!

Buying a salon with freehold property

It is likely to be a bit tricky raising money for such a purchase unless you have some other form of collateral to lodge with the bank as well as the deeds of the salon property. If you are purchasing the business as a first business venture it may be even more hazardous convincing someone to lend you money to purchase this property when you have no proven track record of being able to earn money with your particular skills to repay the loan. It may be difficult but not impossible. However, in all negotiations involving property, do engage the services of two most important people, a property valuer and a solicitor. Find first your solicitor and he will guide you to a good valuer. Do not attempt to ignore the valuer's advice if he warns you that the bricks and mortar of the property are really not worth what the vendor is asking. Negotiate a lower purchase price in keeping with the value your valuer has put on it or look for another salon, but whatever you do don't be misguided into thinking the valuer is wrong.

Buying a business in a leasehold premises

Once again, the most important move you can make when contemplating purchasing a business in a leasehold premises is to engage the services of a good solicitor. The legal tightrope of things that can go wrong with leases can only be really sorted out by him or her. It may be that you are being asked to purchase the remainder of a lease. If so, it must be confirmed exactly how long the lease has left to run, and what the possible intentions of the owner of the property will be when the lease runs out. You may spend the next three years building a wonderful business only to find at the time of re-negotiating a continuing lease, the owner has other plans for the property which does not include you! On the other hand it would possibly include you at a very much higher rent! All these problems could be advised against or minimised by engaging a good solicitor.

Starting from scratch

Many very successful beauty businesses have started out as a completely new venture. A beauty therapist has looked at an area and decided that there were sufficient people around wanting her services and started from there. If this is your idea of a challenge then go ahead, but once again, don't get carried away by enthusiasm. Good ideas don't just happen, they must be backed up by a thorough research of everything that will affect the profitability of the scheme. Walk around in the area, look at the people in the streets, particularly the women. Then ask yourself a whole host of questions. Do they look particularly well dressed? Are there plenty of flourishing hairdressers around? Are the houses well kept? How about the chemist shops, are they stocking only the cheaper brands of cosmetics or do they also have a range of more expensive skin-care products?

Then look at the majority of the people themselves. Are you in 'bed-sit' land where the greatest majority of the population are students? Not much chance of affording beauty treatments on university or college grants. Are you looking at an area which has a large amount of very new, cheaper priced houses for first time buyers and young families with children? Mortgages take up an awful lot of the income when first buying a home. You would be better off looking for premises in an area which serves as a main shopping centre for many of the surrounding suburbs. Your premises might cost you more but at least you would have the advantage of a good cross section of people of all financial abilities and age groups coming into the area. A main road salon which is easily visible and with easy access is a much better proposition than a cheaper premises in a side road which is only seen by people who are actually using the side road. The amount of money you would save on the cheaper premises would be easily swallowed up by very expensive advertising bills to let potential clients know where you are.

What type of premises?

A bright airy salon with plenty of window space for display, preferably sandwiched between an expensive hairdressers and a popular boutique seems to be every therapist's dream of a salon. Unfortunately these are not easily come by and most of the best positions on the high street are already taken by larger companies who can afford extremely high rents. The smaller business companies, particularly the newcomer, must make do with what they can afford. However, if you are lucky enough to find such a shop premises available and the rent seems within your price range then take it, as you will have distinct advantages over any rivals.

If ground floor premises are not available, then the next best thing is to be on the first floor above some retail business. Obviously, it would make life easy if the business on the ground floor was one that was compatible with a beauty salon such as a hairdressers or a ladies' clothes shop, however it need not be. What does make a difference though is if the business downstairs really is not in keeping with the idea of beauty at all, such as a butchers, a hardware or do-it-yourself shop.

Once again a word of warning, if you are contemplating signing a lease for any type of premises consult your solicitor first. If a premises has not been used before as a beauty salon, particularly if it is on the first floor which may have previously been living accommodation, then you may need planning permission for something known as **'change of use'**. Many local authorities are very fussy about this 'change of use' bye-law and if you think that by ignoring it and pleading ignorance, you will get away with it, you won't. Many businesses have had to close down because they have omitted this very important local application.

The local authority has the task of seeing that there is a fair balance of every different type of accommodation available, including commercial and domestic. They are also responsible for overseeing car parking facilities in a particular area. Often planning permission will be granted for 'change of use' provided that the new business makes proper provisions for car parking places for the staff and the long term parking needs of its intended customers. This can sometimes be tricky, especially if your intended premises are on the first or second floor. Any available yard space will surely be taken up by the ground floor tenants. However, look around the immediate area. Nearly all districts have several churches and chapels with a yard attached. Often, if the church or chapel council is approached they will allow weekday parking for certain people in exchange for a regular donation towards the upkeep of the building. Usually they require the car to display a small parking disc. This system can be very convenient to both business and church.

Sharing premises

Many therapists, especially those starting up alone for the first time, find the prospects of finding premises and setting up alone, very daunting. On these occasions it may be more beneficial to consider sharing premises with another business. The most immediate type that springs to mind is the chance of opening a beauty room in a local hairdressing salon. Once again there must be words of caution. However wonderful the idea seems and however friendly the hairdressers and staff are, please make everything on a legal footing. It may be your best friend or even a relative that you intend to share premises with but it is still absolutely imperative to have a legal agreement drawn up so that if or when anything goes wrong, everyone has a certain amount of legal rights. If, for instance, you get on well together for the first couple of years and both businesses flourish and then things go wrong, a few mischosen words can cause an argument and staff taking sides make things worse. A decision has to be made about finding alternative accommodation for the beauty room. OK you leave, but how about your clients if the hairdresser decides to continue with a beauty room and invites someone else to share the premises? Some of your clients would remain loyal and come with you, but many would find it far more convenient to go on visiting the same premises. Therefore you would stand to loose a great deal of your clientele. A carefully worded legal document drawn up at the beginning of the sharing of the premises could restrict the hairdresser from doing just that in the event of such a situation arising.

Hairdressing salons are very suitable for sharing premises with, as are other establishments such as health clubs and sports stadia. In fact any type of concern where the people attending as customers, members or clients are interested in their appearance and health. You can be sure that a large number of them can be converted into regular clients of the beauty salon.

Renting a chair

The idea of renting a chair has become popular in recent years in hairdressing. Young stylists who cannot afford the expense of a salon on their own, pay to rent a chair and reception facilities. This situation, however, becomes fraught with problems and many a young person has built up a good clientele only to find that a difference of opinion with the owner leaves him out in the cold with no business and seemingly no legal compensations. Advertisements are now appearing offering the same facilities for beauty therapists. Anyone contemplating this kind of arrangement is strongly advised to consult a solicitor and have some form of legal protection drawn up before embarking on such a scheme.

There are, however, many other professionals compatible with beauty therapy, such as dentists, opticians, physiotherapists and chiropodists, but these usually prefer to restrict their consulting rooms to the practice of electrolysis or remedial camouflage.

Parking facilities

Finding the right premises may be an extremely difficult job, but finding the right premises with available easy parking near at hand is almost impossible, but absolutely necessary. If the business is to get off the ground and be a success the main consideration when viewing potential premises has to be parking facilities. The largest percentage of clientele drive themselves. Nobody will want to attend the salon if, afterwards, she has to walk through terrible weather to get back to her car. Only in the very large cities, such as London, where the general public are used to using taxis, can one contemplate a premises that does not have a car park near at hand.

Back to a plan again: salon layout

Having found your ideal premises, or as near ideal as you can afford, and reassured yourself that it has adequate parking potentials, it is time to return to a plan again. This time you need pencil and paper to work out the proposed inside layout. Even if only one person, yourself, will be working the salon at first, it is necessary to plan carefully the exact layout so that you will be involved in the minimum amount of walking around to reach the various things you will need. List at the top of your plan the essential working areas and then roughly map out where they will be. Obviously a reception area will be as near to the entrance as possible, and this is usually coupled with a small waiting area and a place for clients to leave their coats.

If a full beauty therapy service is being offered you will need a facial room or cubicle, a body treatment area, complete with a 'wet' section, ie a non-carpeted area where steam bath or sauna or similar body heating equipment can be sited. It is a good idea, if space is limited, to place the waxing unit in this area. A shower unit is another essential item, particularly if sun-bed facilities are offered.

Although in the early planning stages you know that it will be only you working in it, all plans must include provisions for other staff. Therefore do not make the mistake of taking on premises which are obviously on the very small side unless you have the option to rent more as you expand. Many salons have started small with only the owner/operator and then, in a very short while, wished they had walls made of elastic. On the other hand, do not take on too large a space. Remember that all space has to have rent and rates paid on it and it will also need to be heated.

It is so difficult to generalise on how the available space should be divided up because each individual premises will be different. A large open plan space will have to be cubicled off in order to afford privacy to the individual clients. This can be done in several ways but the more popular methods are either light weight hardboard or louvred panels fixed to the floors and used as walls with a curtain over the entrance or all curtained cubicles with the curtains suspended from custom-built tracking, such as in hospitals. The latter method is very useful if one keeps in mind the possibility of making large cubicles to begin with which can then be subdivided when further staff are engaged.

The main walls of the salon should be painted or papered in a very light colour or white to reflect as much light as possible. The choice of curtain material is very much to the taste of the individual but bear in mind that very light curtains show every finger mark and darker shades can be a bit intimidating, particularly in a smaller cubicle. Heavy patterning can also feel oppressive and lines and squares on the curtains positively jump off the fabric at you after you have been working in them for some time! The decor or theme of the salon will obviously have to reflect the area in which you intend working. An elegant regency style or even an art deco style would be appropriate if your salon is situated in one of the wealthier parts of town, but would probably be very off-putting if you tried those styles in a predominently working class area. In these areas, the successful salons are those which are open and inviting with a simple modern theme.

On your plan, arrange very carefully sufficient sources of hot and cold water. If it is necessary to call in the plumber to fit a shower and wash-hand-basin, decide now if one of each will be sufficient in the near future. Not only will it be cheaper to have all plumbing needs done at the same time but it will also save having the salon closed in precious working time in the future when further washing facilities are needed. This also applies to your electrical needs. When plotting out each cubicle, bear in mind that it will be necessary to have at least one piece of electrical equipment plugged in when in use as well as possibly another source of light such as a lamp or illuminated magnifier. A minimum of two wall sockets are absolutely essential for each working cubicle or room.

A stock room which can also double up as a staff room and kitchen is also essential. This will help keep all unsightly muddles out of sight and give the salon a clean and light, uncluttered look. Plenty of good, clear mirrors at every vantage point, both full length and short ones, complete the planning of the empty salon.

Equipment to buy or to lease?

Basically a beauty therapist should be able to perform a great deal of her treatments with only the skill of her hands, but even so a minimum of equipment would still be needed. The first major consideration must be something for the client either to lie or sit on. A reclining beauty chair with all the refinements of a hydraulic lifting system and adjustable headrest, or a traditional consulting room couch/massage bed?

The beauty chairs are superb when doing any type of facial or electrolysis but, despite some of them being advertised as capable of converting to a massage couch for body treatments, this can only be done with difficulty. Particularly if the client is rather a heavyweight. In this instance a massage couch is by far the best for the job. If it has an adjustable head, as most of them do, then this can also be used for facial work. When finances are strictly limited, then the massage couch may be the best choice because of its versatility. If, however, space is very limited, the beauty chair may have to be first choice as it does not take up so much room. A telephone call to some of the companies listed at the end of the book will bring a flood of beautifully illustrated leaflets showing a wonderful variety of

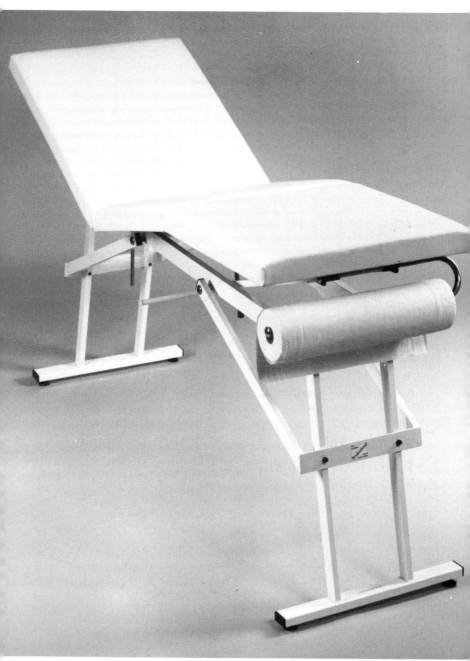

The beauty massage couch must look elegant as well as be functional. The better ones incorporate a paper roll holder for hygienic covering using disposable paper roll

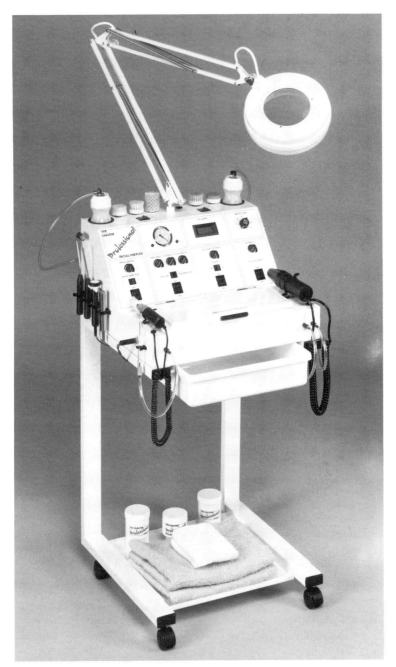

Where space is at a premium, this compact unit is a must. This version contains: galvanic, high frequency, brush cleansing, vacuum massage and fine sprays. Complemented by the cold light magnifyer and the useful storage drawer

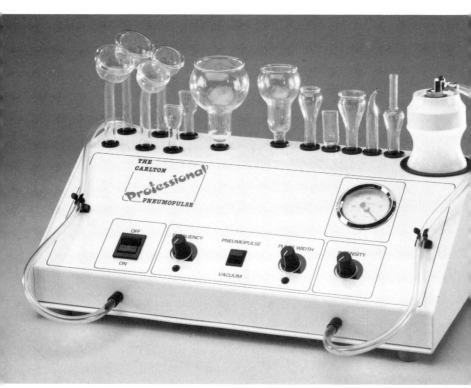

A sophisticated vacuum machine which also incorporates a pneumopulse, with an easy-to-read pressure gauge. Invaluable in a busy facial clinic where a wide variety of treatments are offered

really well designed equipment. Even so it would be advisable to follow up this browsing with a personal visit to the showrooms. Sit on the chairs, lie on the couches, and really look over all the equipment thoroughly. Remember it will have to last a long time before you will be able to replace it. If it has to earn your living for you, it must be sturdy, neat and stylish as well as easily cleanable. Try not to purchase any equipment that has difficult corners which could trap dirt and look unsightly. Even in the best organised salons, machines can get knocks and bumps, so do make sure your purchases will be able to

A sturdy floor standing multi-directional lamp complete with small magnifying screen. Useful in all parts of the salon but an essential item in the make-up studios

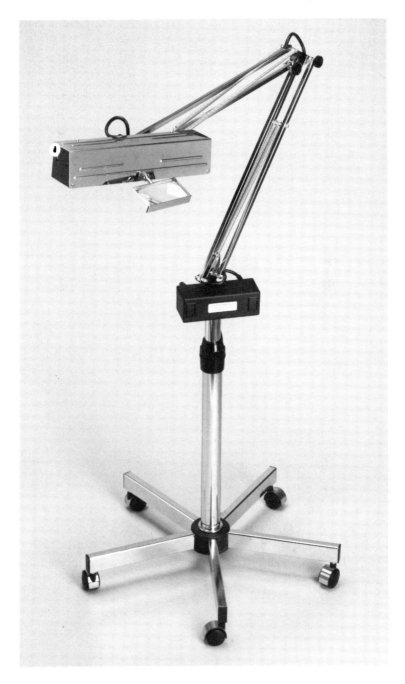

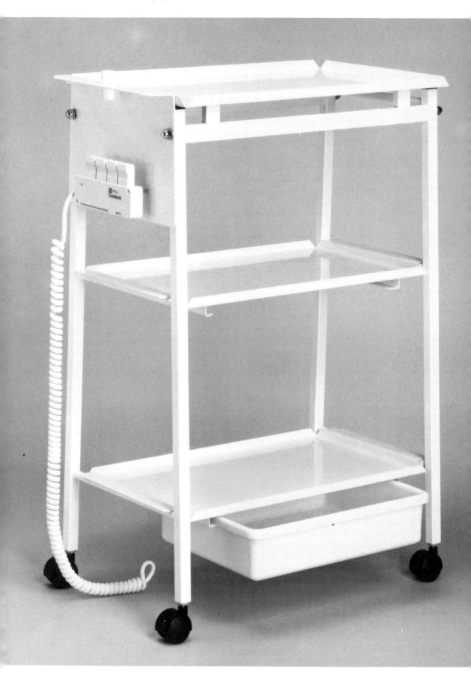

withstand constant use. Nothing is worse in a busy salon than an essential item of equipment always being at the repair shop. This is why the more expensive piece of equipment to purchase initially may end up by being the cheapest in the long run. If it is solidly built and with a good service back-up offered by the manufacturer, it may well outlive by two or three times some of the cheaper copies of the same machine.

New or second-hand?

If the amount of money available for the initial setting up of the salon is severely limited, it is possible to furnish the salon with the bare essentials bought second-hand. It requires a great deal of patience, scanning the local papers daily looking for such bargains but they do occur as other salons either upgrade their equipment or unfortunately go out of business. The professional journals often carry advertisements for such items, but it is necessary to be on the phone as soon as you see them as they all seem to get snapped up quickly. When purchasing second-hand, do take care. Examine things very carefully, insist on seeing everything working and, if possible, ask to see original receipts as this will confirm the age of the different pieces of equipment. With most second-hand items it would be a useful guide to reckon on paying not more than half of the original price. This is a very rough guide as much will depend on the age and condition of the particular item.

Hire purchase or leasing?

Hire purchase facilities are available through most of the large equipment suppliers. This requires you to pay a certain percentage of the purchase price as a deposit and the remainder in monthly instalments. This is quite a good method of purchasing but it must be remembered that the instalments must be paid whether the salon is taking money or not. Also

Modern multi-purpose trolley with electrical sockets for several pieces of equipment to be used simultaneously. A useful drawer keeps small equipment clean and tidy

interest has to be paid which makes each item you purchase much more expensive in the long run.

There is also a method of obtaining equipment known as 'leasing'. Using this method the equipment is delivered to the salon on receipt of the first three months' payment in advance. There is then a set monthly charge for a specified period of time, sometimes two years, sometimes three. During that time the equipment remains the property of the leasing company and normally they have a servicing agreement in which they undertake to keep the equipment in good working order for the length of the leasing period. At the end of that time the equipment is then offered to the salon at a nominal sum, sometimes as low as £1. This method has its advantages, particularly when the salon is well established with a full appointment book meaning a steady income with which to pay the monthly instalments.

Whichever method is used to finance the purchases, the main thing is to choose carefully and cautiously.

Keeping things ticking

As all the equipment we use in the salons is powered by electricity great care must be taken to ensure safety in use, not only for the sake of the client but also for the well being of the therapist. Some of the larger equipment houses offer a servicing agreement on equipment which has been purchased new from them. This servicing agreement may be expensive but does give an efficient back up in the care and safety of the equipment. Where this is not available it makes sound sense to find a local electrician, qualified to work with our types of machines, and make some local arrangements for regular servicing.

The therapist herself can save a lot of money by using her common sense and maintaining the equipment properly and not abusing it. For the sake of safety all the machines must be fitted with the correct type of fused plug and only one piece of equipment at a time should be fitted into each socket. All leads and wires should be examined regularly to ensure that nothing is damaged or fraying. It is also a good policy to ensure that all the leads to the machines, particularly when they are plugged in and working, are not left trailing across the floor where other people can fall over them. Thinking '*safety*' protects not only the client but the staff as well.

Protection by insurance

Insurances are one of those maddening things that we all hate to pay for but, when needed, we are glad to have them. When money is scarce at the setting up of a new business it is an awful temptation to think that we can work for a few months without the added expense of insurance, but beware! That is the time when you are sure to need it. In the salon there are several different types of insurance, but everyone of them is vitally necessary.

There is actually only one form of insurance which is obligatory by law and that is the **Employers' Liability Insurance**. Even if you only have a domestic assistant coming into clean for a few hours or a young Saturday morning girl to help with the tea, you must have the Employers' Liability Insurance. It is not expensive, but without it you can be fined quite heavily, not only for not having it, but also a back fine for every day you had an employee on the premises without cover! Therefore if nothing else, this one is a must!

The next important form of insurance is the **Professional Indemnity Insurance**. This protects the client from any form of damage you may do to her during a treatment or as a result of a treatment, and no self respecting therapist should work without this cover. Normally this would be a very expensive insurance to negotiate if it were left to each individual therapist to make her own arrangements with an insurance company. Thanks, however, to the good work of the main professional organisations, who have negotiated on behalf of their members, Professional Indemnity Insurance can be obtained quite easily through membership of the organisations and at a reasonable cost. Obviously this insurance depends on the therapist being a properly qualified and professional person who abides by the Code of Ethics of her organisation.

The Professional Indemnity Insurance, however, only covers a client for damage caused by professional negligence, it does not protect us against claims made by a client who damages or injures herself in any way when on our premises. For this type of cover we need the Public Liability Insurance.

The final insurance necessary is that of insuring our premises, stock and equipment against damage fire and theft. This sounds an awful lot of insurance premiums to be paying out. Nothing however, compared to what we might be paying if there was any trouble and we didn't have the protection of the insurance companies.

6 Salon success

The treatment brochure: What will you put on your menu?

The new salon having been painted and decorated, designed with a place for everything, the task now is to decide what to do with it. A beauty salon is not just a pretty room with lots of luxurious chairs in it. Life and energy has to be breathed into it by a beauty therapist who knows what she is doing, and more to the point, knows what her potential clientele will want in the way of treatments.

Like a good restaurant, the new beauty salon must have a wide and varied 'menu' of treatments in order to attract the maximum number of clients of all age groups. The more treatments you have on offer the more likely you are to be a success but remember most of the treatments will involve capital expenditure on either equipment or materials. Therefore it is essential that the treatment list be planned as effectively and as detailed as possible.

Old faithfuls: classic treatments

Draft out your treatment list with the six or seven standard classic treatments, such as facials, manicure, pedicure, eyelash tinting, leg waxing, body massage, and electrolysis. Then start to elaborate. Take for instance the facials. With the purchase of just one good machine, you can extend your range to include:

1 desincrustation facial
2 iontophoresis facial

3 high frequency facial (using direct method)
4 high frequency facial (using indirect method).

While still including a basic facial, using no electricity at all for those clients who would prefer it that way, you can list on your printed brochure at least five facials. All of these different electrical features can now be obtained in one machine.

The same can apply to the body treatments. Buy equipment which has several applications. The better quality galvanic machines have not only the two different galvanic methods for the face, and high frequency but also a galvanic body treatment. Always look for equipment that has this kind of versatility. Not only is it cheaper than buying many different machines, but also it is economical on space when the salon is smaller than average. If space as well as finances are limited, consider a steam bath and sun-bed as your two forms of wet and dry heat rather than the space consuming, and expensive to buy, saunas. Start with one sun-bed, the best quality you can get, but be prepared to need another one pretty soon as this is a very popular form of salon treatment.

With the inclusion of sun-beds in practically every sports complex up and down the country, it was considered at one time that sun-beds would not retain their popularity in salons, but this has proved to be unfounded. A salon which offers a properly supervised sun-bed facility, with strict standards of hygiene and adequate shower facilities can still attract a large number of discerning clients who prefer the more private salon environment.

Body massage is also a very popular treatment, but if you can afford the extra training to take in **aromatherapy** body massage as well, you can maximise your massage skills and extend your range of body treatments.

Manicure can be the standard treatment and then, for the price of a block of paraffin wax, a luxury wax treatment for the hands, can be listed. The same can apply with pedicure. Advertise not only your standard treatment but also the more expensive wax pedicure. Obviously the wax treatments will be priced higher to include, as well as the cost of the wax, the extra time taken in preparing and applying it.

A sure-fire way to keep the salon busy both summer and winter is to include **electrolysis** in your scheme of work. In the chapter on training it is stressed that this facet of the beauty therapist's work is extremely important and this will be very apparent right from the start of any new venture. A good, careful, gentle, caring electrologist will soon make her name in any area and be in great demand. This, of course, brings clients into the salon who then convert to other treatments as well.

New treatments can always be added to your range, as and when you can afford the extra equipment or materials needed. Some treatments are more popular than others but they vary from salon to salon. A recent survey showed that the 'Top Ten' in order of popularlity are:

1 Electrolysis	6 Body treatments
2 Waxing	7 Suntanning
3 Facials	8 Aromatherapy
4 Eyelash tint	9 Pedicure
5 Manicure	10 Reflexology

Price list or brochure?

Because of the very expensive costs of new artwork and layout, the quotes one gets for a well-produced brochure makes the mind boggle. The temptation to make do with a single sheet typed price list is very great, but do not skimp on this very important item. Remember you are a new salon, and nobody has heard of you, so first impressions count a great deal. Create as much of an impact as you can on the minds of potential clients by presenting yourself and the new salon as the experts.

To the uninitiated new client, a plain list of facials listed in a line, all with different prices, means nothing. Neither does the list of facials we have drawn up here. The average lady hasn't a clue what an iontophoresis facial is, let alone wanting to have one. So plan your brochure very carefully explaining in layman's terms just what you are offering.

Take for instance our example of the iontophoresis facial, how much more interesting to your client if she can read:

Rejuvenation facial . . . Pamper yourself with the luxury of an hour-long facial designed for the more mature skin. The face and neck are cleansed, massaged by hand, a masque is applied, following by a collagen ampoule to stimulate the skin into regenerating itself. Very fine wrinkles are puffed out and the skin feels soft and refreshed. Designed to help retard the ageing process . . . Price £XX

Or perhaps you expect to attract a large number of under 25's? Why not offer:

Problem Skin Special . . . A problem shared is a problem halved, why not let our experienced therapists help you with yours. Our Problem Skin Special offers you a gentle cleansing peel of the dead layer on your skins surface, followed by an electrical desincrustation which will bring out most of the impurities in the skin. These are then removed by the use of an extractor and any blackheads near the surface will be gently eased out. This is then followed by a masque designed to stabilise the acid/alkaline balance of the skin leaving it soft and clear.

The idea is to catch the prospective clients imagination and let her picture herself being on the receiving end of such pampering. However, don't be too enthusiastic and get carried away. Always remember the **Trade Description Act** is waiting to catch anyone who over exaggerates on such literature. Never, never promise to make anyone look, younger or different when you know it cannot be done. Carefully word any brochure statements only with claims you know you can substantiate.

All this sounds very complicated and time consuming, but while solicitors and valuers are sorting out leases and such, then is the time for you to be planning exactly what you will be able to offer. The range you intend doing will also depend on how much space you have available as well as equipment.

Printing your masterpiece

Having really thought out this brochure very carefully, bearing in mind that it is cheaper to have thousands printed rather than hundreds, the next step is to find a good printer. Although the *Yellow Pages* are full of them, it is quite a task finding one that will both take the work on, give a reasonable cost quote, and also be reasonably prompt with the work. For some reason or other, printers would appear to be the most overworked people under the sun. Ask to see a mock up of the finished brochure. Some will try to talk you into expensive vellum or card but quite honestly a good quality A4 paper, printed on both sides, and then folded into three (see illustration), will be quite sufficient. The front will obviously be taken up with the name of the salon and the address, and if the owner is qualified it looks impressive to have the name of the owner/or manageress complete with professional qualifications.

When discussing your brochure with the printers, many will not warn you that it must contain the prices of the treatments. If it doesn't it will be classed simply as a brochure and will attract VAT at the current rate. If it contains the prices of treatments, then it will be classed as a price list, regardless of how elaborate or involved it is and will accordingly escape VAT. Your first order from your new printer will be much more expensive than any subsequent order because it will include what printers refer to as setting up artwork. This why it makes sense to return to the same printer, provided that you are satisfied with his work, so that he already has your 'plates' prepared. Whichever way you do it, it is an expensive commodity but, as stated before, it is *so* important to create a good impression right from the start. With all these expenses it is imperative to keep a file handy into which the receipts and quotes for all work done must be placed. Start off with tidy and organised habits so that when you need to re-order anything, or when the end of your first financial year comes, all receipts for money spent are readily available.

Beauty Within

111-119 REGENT STREET
KINGSWOOD
BRISTOL

Telephone: Bristol 672823

FIGURE CORRECTION TREATMENTS

Standard Figure Trimming
¼ hour vacuum massage to help break down stubborn fat deposits followed by electronic muscle toning.
1 hour   £

Electronic Muscle Toning
A treatment designed to tighten and firm slack muscles works wonders after losing weight or childbirth.
1 hour   £

"Cellulite Treatment"
G 5, heavy duty vibrator followed by vacuum massage, ideal for thick thighs and buttocks.
½ hour   £

Manicure   £

Pedicure   £

Chiropody treatment available on request.

Ear Piercing
Complete with 24ct gold plated studs   £

MASSAGE

Steam Bath and Massage
A wonderful form of relaxation therapy beginning with a relaxing steam bath, followed by Swedish hand massage.
£

Steam Bath, Massage and Relaxatron
This is the standard massage treatment followed by a session on the Relaxatron vibratory couch. A marvellous therapy for nervous tension.
£

Aromatherapy Massage
A steam bath to relax you followed by an expert massage of the whole body using Aromatherapy Oils.
£

Stimulating G.5 Massage
A stimulating massage using the heavy duty vibrating G.5. Tones the muscles, helps break down fat deposits and "wakes up" a sluggish circulation.
£

Steam Bath only   £

Remedial Massage and other alternative therapies available on request.

All figure trimming treatments are guided by our expert advice on diets and exercising

The treatments in this Salon are exclusively for Ladies. We regret we have no facilities for men

Consultant Beauty Therapist

JOY MORRIS F S B Th. M A B T
Member of the British Association of Beauty Therapy and Cosmetology

BEAUTY FOR YOUR FACE

Deep Cleanse and Make-up only.
Suitable for Weddings, Parties or that Special
Occasion   £

Regeneration Facial

Deep Cleanse, eyebrow shaping, face
massage, masque designed for your skin
type, toning and moisturising.   £

Make-up extra   £

Problem Skin Facial

We are now able to offer 'Galvanic
Desincrustation, facials for the skin which
is excessively oily with blackheads and
blocked pores
Also suitable for teenage and adult acne.
                                            £

Rejuvenation Facial

Designed to aid the normal, dry, or mature
skin, using 'Iontophoresis'. This aids the
absorption of special creams to a much
deeper level of the skin, thereby puffing out
fine lines and wrinkles   £

Aromatherapy Facial

The facial which concentrates on treating the
face with the art of hand massage, using
Essential Oils'. These expensive, exclusive
oils put back the bloom of youth into ageing or
neglected skins   £

To compliment the beauty treatments of
the Salon, Beauty Within are pleased to offer
you our own designed beauty skin care range.
All the creams and lotions contain only the
purest ingredients and are not tested on
animals in any way.

Always available are —

Wild Rose Deep Cleanser
Wild Rose Toning Lotion
Light Moisture Cream
Avocado Nourishing Cream
Herbal Toning Lotion
Wild Thyme Toning Lotion
Aromatherapy Body Oil

Other products are being researched and
will be available later.

Electrolysis

This is the only permanent method of
removing unwanted hair from the face, legs
or body. All treatments carried out by fully
qualified, expert staff using the new gamma
sterilised disposable needle.

¼ hour   £
½ hour   £

Eyebrow Re-Styling   from   £

Eyelash and Eyebrow tinting

Do away with the chore of applying mascara,
eyelashes can be tinted either black, brown,
grey or blue or blue/black. Tinting makes
lashes look longer

Lashes only   £
Brows only   £
Brows and lashes   £

Wax Epilation

Hair on face removed by cool wax method

Upper lip   £
Chin area   £

Leg Waxing

Full leg and bikini line   £
Half leg   £
Bikini line   £
Under arm wax   £

Naming the salon

Thinking up a name for this new salon will sure to be a traumatic experience unless you have a good mind for this kind of game. The name must convey images to the client, so you have to be sure that you are conveying the right image. Even if your name is Fifi and you intend doing body massage for ladies only, if you call it 'Fifi's Massage Parlour' then you know that you are going to attract very unwanted attentions. On the other hand, try not to be so conservative that it becomes boring. Also watch out for unfortunate word associations. There are several beauty salons around the country that call themselves 'The Beauty Spot' or 'Betty's Beauty Spot'. In many people's minds, by word association, the word 'spot' means a large red, nasty lump on the face. This surely is not the image they hoped to convey! Try to juggle with words to paint a mental picture. Nothing too pompous but on the other hand nothing too humorous or the salon, and the work done in it, will not gain much respect. You can, of course, include your own name, but honestly, only if it bears any weight. When the very well know therapist, Joan Price, opened her salon in London, the name Joan Price's Face Place was just right. People knew who Joan Price was and immediately accepted that this was a salon that specialised in facial and cosmetic work. However, little Betty Boop is so far an unknown personality, and anyway 'The Face Place' is Joan's trade mark so don't try to copy it. Try to do as Joan did and think of something as original as you can and make it exclusively yours.

I believe that beauty comes from within and also my newest salon is housed within another larger premises so the obvious choice was to call this latest salon 'Beauty Within'. A name that conveys two messages, which ever way you look at it.

Give this new business name as much thought as you would to naming a child. It is your child and you have to live with the name of it around you, you hope, for some time to come.

The great problem which puzzles many new owners is if they are, quite unwittingly, stealing someone else's trade name. You may, of course, call yours 'Betty Boop's Beauty Salon' because it is unlikely thtat there will be another Betty Boop in a beauty salon, but if you decide to call it anything other than your own name then you are obliged to register the made up name with **The Registrar of Business Names**, 2nd Floor, Companies House, 55–71 City Road, London EC1Y 2DN.

At one time it was obligatory to register a business name, then came a time when it was rescinded, but I am given to understand that the Registry is back in business again and for one's own protection it is wise to register your carefully thought out name. If nothing else, it protects you from someone else who thinks it is a good name and decides to call their new salon by the same name. It is an offence knowingly to attempt to use someone else's business name even if they are not in the same line as you, particularly if that name is a famous one or they can prove in court that it is theirs. Also you cannot dream up a name that implies you are a larger company than you are. International Beauty Therapy Inc would immediately conjure up the suggestion that the company had beauty business ventures throughout the world, so you would not be allowed to get away with that across the front of a little high street salon fascia.

Neither can you normally choose a name that suggests you have any connections with the Crown or royalty. There are, of course, always exceptions, such as the company called Queen Cosmetics Ltd. Their name is perfectly legal because it is their registered trade mark and has been so since the business was first started in 1927, long before there was any legal regulations in force about not using such a title. The company is, quite understandably, very proud of its unique name.

A letter of enquiry to the above address of the Register of Business Names will soon bring a reply clarifying the situation for you, but in the meantime do not go ahead with any printing as it could be a costly process to have to change the name.

Advertising and public relations

Sometimes thought by some people to be the same thing, but your accountant will tell you they definitely are not. **Advertis-**

ing costs you money, lots of it, and doesn't always bring in as much new work as you had hoped it would. **Public relations**, on the other hand, is not completely free but it can sometimes be far more effective than advertising. The difficulty is, however much we object to the huge sums of money we have to spend on it, advertising is a must at the opening of a new salon. It is no good approaching your local newspapers telling them about the opening of your new salon in the fond hope that they will do a feature on it just because it is new and revolutionary in your little corner of the world. Unless you are prepared to advertise with them then they will not be interested. But in all fairness, if you do agree to spend money on advertising with them, they will often arrange to do a 'feature', especially if they can persuade other people who have been involved with the preparation of the new salon, such as the plumber, electrical contractor and equipment supplier, also to take advertising space. This could have the desired effect and bring new clients flocking in, but if you are in an area well served with other beauty establishments, it might not. You may have to do other things to attract attention. Another word of warning; offering to do free treatment for one of the female journalists does not always work out the way you envisage.

At the opening of a new beauty school the owners made such an offer to the largest newspaper in their area and the 'Womens' Page' editor was despatched to the school to sample their delights. Despite spending hundreds of pounds with the newspaper on advertising the new school owners were horrified to read, a few days later, the most flippant article that really ridiculed the whole of the serious business of beauty therapy training.

Your opening advertisement should be pleasing to the eye but also contain as much information to the prospective client as possible. Once you have prepared your advertising copy, read and re-read it to ensure that it really tells the client everything she wants to know. Make sure you have the telephone number in big, bold print so that all she has to do is pick up the phone and dial.

One of the best value for money advertisements is the *Yellow*

Pages. Your business telephone account will automatically give you a small entry under the classified heading of Beauty Salons but if you want another entry, say much larger with a box around it, or you want an entry under another classification, such as Electrologists, then you will have to pay more. These extra entries are expensive but they do keep your name in front of the general public. *Yellow Pages* directories last for ages but one issue of the morning or evening paper is invariably thrown away the next day. There is nothing so dead as yesterday's newspaper. Maximise your chance of your advertisement being seen by as many people as possible by considering every angle of advertising so that you can use the money you have allocated as effectively as possible.

Public relations, can you afford them?

Public relations is a very different form of advertising but one that you really cannot ignore. Public relations is the view that the general public has of you and your little salon. It can make or break you, and so great care must be taken to present the best possible image at all times. Even the choice of a name for the salon is part of a public relations campaign. If you have the name wrong and the public get the wrong impression of you then you have poor public relations. Being seen to be a very professional and caring salon, always doing the ethically correct thing, is good public relations. Offering a speaker for women's clubs in the area, giving prizes of treatments for the latest charity fund raising event, anything which brings your name and the name of the salon to the notice of the public in a favourable way is good for the salon. A form of good public relations, and the most effective method of advertising is one that many therapists tend to overlook. It is giving the best possible, ethically correct, treatment that you can give to existing clients. There is no better advertisement for any form of business than a satisfied customer. If you please a client then she will immediately go out and tell a whole circle of other people. Sisters, friends, colleagues at work, they all hear about you and your good treatment. Even if you have had to refuse to perform a certain treatment on a client because she is contra-indicated, invariably she will recruit more clients for you. The message will go out among her circle that you cared enough about her well-being, not to perform the treatments she asked for, and even explained carefully why you could not do it. This immediately raises you in their eyes as being a person of integrity who would prefer to loose a fee rather than perform an unsuitable treatment. You can't get better advertising than that even if you took out a whole-page advertisement.

Show a pretty face

The front of your premises should also be made as eye catching as possible and tastefully decorated. It should attract attention and make the passing woman in the street want to come in. It is sometimes a mistake to appear to be so exclusive and expensive that you drive the majority of potential clients away. Try to achieve a happy medium. If you are on an upper floor then arrange your windows and curtains as attractively and invitingly as you can. Most upstairs premises have some use of either a display window or a display cabinet on the front of the building or in the entrance. Arrange to have some first class photographs taken of the interior of the salon and display them somewhere on street level. If you intend retailing a range of cosmetics, then advertising material from the manufacturer will also help to make a good visual display and get the salon noticed. Do resist the temptation to put up hand written notices on windows and doors. Get some printed by the professionals, or failing that make a really good job yourself by purchasing sets of stick-on lettering from any good stationers and carefully measuring the card so that all the letters spelling out your message are neatly in line.

Now go to the other side of the road and take a long, slow, critical look at your premises. Would it really appeal to you? Does it draw your attention like a magnet? If not, why not? Perhaps it is too nondescript? Use your imagination in making it outstanding. If your are lucky enough to have a display window, then go to town on your opening display. If you haven't a clue where to start then take a ride up to town and wander around looking at all the big store windows, preferably when they are closed but when all their lights are on. See how the professionals go about it. You will find those that please the eye most will be the ones that are simple and uncluttered but extremely effective. Observe how the dresser has blended ranges of colours, usually to coincide with a new season or something special. Colours are never put in regardless. They are always ranged with complementary colours and textures. Now go back and try something similar.

Beginners blues

The salon is all ready and waiting, with the windows well decorated, announcing your great day of opening. Advertisements have appeared in the local press, the telephone is installed. All you have to do is stand by and wait for the rush! Don't be surprised that instead of feeling elated and on top of the world you feel as though judgement day is fast approaching! Every caring person gets such a feeling. The terrible thought that the clients may not come. You may have spent all that money and will look a fool when you cannot repay the bank.

The answer is to keep busy, keep smiling, be pleasant, and slowly and surely the clients will trickle in. Sometimes a grand opening with free wine will initially bring a crowd in, but that does not necessarily mean they will make good regular clients who will pay for your bread and butter. Party celebrations are better if they are kept for the first, second and subsequent birthdays of a successful business. Opening day is much better if it is a quiet professional affair which gives intending customers the impression that you are there for the very serious business of helping them with their problems. After all that is what a beauty salon is all about.

New ideas

As the salon gets busier and busier it is a good idea to be on the look out for different treatments to enlarge your range. Avoid, if possible, the gimmicky type of miracle treatment which invariably crops up from time to time. Study the professional journals, attend seminars and conferences, go on refresher courses. Always be trying to upgrade your own knowledge so that you can offer the best possible service to your clients.

This is also the best way of fighting competition. Being able to offer the widest range of treatments possible, will ensure that your clients are not tempted to go elsewhere. You may not have any competition to begin with but you can be sure that the minute you have built your business up successfully, someone else will try and muscle in on you and attempt to attract your clients away. Don't be dismayed by this or resort to dirty tricks. Simply ignore the competition and go on giving the highest standard you can.

Time for two? First employee

Deciding when the salon is busy enough to take on someone else besides yourself is a tricky problem. It depends a great deal on how much of your own time you are prepared to devote to working. However, when you are completely full all day long and find that you are unable to cope with the constant interruptions of the telephone and reception as well as doing the treatments, then is the time to consider engaging someone to help.

Think very carefully whether it is more help with the reception and telephone work you need, or another pair of fully qualified hands. If you are thinking of employing someone to do just reception work then do realise that the income of the salon is not going to rise by very much. Your life will be made easier but there will still only be the one pair of hands working. This can be helped somewhat by ensuring that you engage someone who is not only capable of doing reception work, but can sell as well. This way she can take over and hopefully build up your retail sales side of the business.

It is more than likely that you will be so inundated with clients that you will realise that it makes sound sense to engage another qualified person to take over some of your workload.

In that case it is sensible to decide that you can both take it in turns to cope with the reception and telephone. Now comes the tricky problem of finding someone who is suitably qualified and with whom you think you may be happy working. More to the point, not only have you to like her but the clients have also to be considered. Then comes the thorny problem, do you take someone straight from college who, because she does not have experience, will not expect such a high wage or do you ask for someone experienced and be prepared to pay a higher wage?

Remember when working out what you think the business could afford to pay her in salary that you not only have to pay her when she is working, but she will also be entitled to paid holidays after a certain period, so there will be weeks when she has to be paid with no money coming into the till. Also, as well as her salary you must pay a *National Insurance* contribution towards her stamp. The minute you have any employee, paid or unpaid, on the premises then you are legally liable to provide Employers' Liability Insurance. Before your first employee actually joins you it is imperative that you notify the Income Tax inspector. He will arrange for a set of instructions to be sent to you so that you will be ready to deduct Pay As You Earn Income Tax from her first weeks wage. This deduction, along with her National Insurance contribution, and yours towards her stamp, has to be sent monthly to the Collector of Taxes. At first sight, the Income Tax forms make the whole task look very formidable, but after a few weeks it becomes a relatively simple task.

Choosing the right person

An advertisement in the local paper or a telephone call to the local job centre will usually produce a good crop of applications. If you ask for someone with experience, be prepared to find the inexperienced applying as well. If you have trained locally yourself and know the staff at your old college well, it would make sense to approach them and ask if they know of anyone who is looking for a place. They may well be able to recommend someone. It is a good idea to reserve a half day if possible for interviewing and see everyone who applies with the right qualifications on the same day. Look very carefully at her appearance and grooming. Then try to assess her personality. Of course, this is not always possible in one interview as people are often nervous and not giving a good picture of themselves. If she is a chatterbox, consider if that would drive you mad after working with her for a few hours. Also, would her chattering disturb the clients? On the other hand is she too quiet? Is that quietness sullen and moody? Could you work with someone that sulked?

As important as her personality is her work. It is a good idea to recruit a few friends to come along as models and ask her to do a few treatments for you to see how she works. However, that should not really be necessary if she has attained the pass standard of the acceptable examination boards.

When you have finally decided on the right person for you and your salon, be sure to state that you will take her on for a trial period, say for one month. At the end of that time she must be told if she is suitable and if so she must be given, by law, a **Contract of Employment** which sets out all the important and relevant points about her employment. The contract must state clearly her hours, holidays and other conditions of employment. It is a good idea to have this form of contract drawn up by your solicitor and have added into it a clause which prohibits her from working for anyone else or herself within a certain distance radius of your salon if and when she leaves you. This is perfectly legal and helps deter people from working for you, getting to know all your clientele and then leaving to set themselves up in business opposite you and canvassing all your clients. This happens so frequently and nearly every time that it does, it could have been prevented by this very simple clause in the contract.

Hopefully this will be the beginning of a very good working relationship. It is not necessary to be bossy and officious to be a good employer, as long as you tell your employee exactly what you expect of her and then let her get on with the work. It is a great temptation in the early days to want to watch her to make sure that she is doing the treatments correctly. Please resist this temptation as this will not bring out the best in your staff. You must respect their professional ability the same as you would expect them to respect yours. As long as you are fair and don't expect them to do anything that you can't do yourself, things should go well. Try to maintain a happy atmosphere as this will reflect throughout the salon and the clients will be aware of it. Nothing will drive your clients away faster than a bad atmosphere. A good atmosphere, honest and sensible treatments and an attractive salon with caring staff is the blue print for success in Beauty Therapy.

Whichever part of the world of beauty you choose to work in, it is hoped that this book will be of some help in making yours a happy and rewarding career.

APPENDIX

Books for further reading

The following is a list of books which any beauty therapist would find very interesting as they are so varied and provide the reader with a different viewpoint. Although one may not necessarily agree with that viewpoint it is essential that the good beauty therapist should be as well informed as possible and be aware of every school of thought on the various subject matters with which we are concerned in our daily work. This is by no means a fully comprehensive list of all the books available, just a suggested selection.

To keep abreast of the new developments in the profession it is essential that one attends conferences, seminars and demonstrations in order to be aware of what is going on. The professional organisations play a great part in keeping their members well informed and membership of these organisations also brings news and views by way of their own journals.

The monthly magazine *Health and Beauty Salon*, under the expert editorship of Ms Marian Mathews, helps enormously in keeping the working therapist in touch with the wider world of beauty therapy and is recommended reading.

ALLEN, M, *The Joy of Slimming*, Wolfe 1974
BASRA, D, *The Ageing Skin*, Diva 1986
BEARD, G, *Massage Principles and Techniques*
BUCHMAN, H, *Stage Make-up*, Pitman 1971
CRONIN, E, *Contact Dermatitis*, Churchill Livingstone 1980
DEVI, I, *Yoga for You*, Thomas 1960
EMERALD, J, *Make-up in Movies, Drama and Photography*
FERRIMAN, D, *Human Hair Growth in Health and Disease*, Thomas 1971
GALLANT, A, *Body treatments and dietetics for the Beauty Therapist*, Stanley Thorns

GALLANT, A, *Principles and Techniques for the Beauty Therapist*, Stanley Thorns 1983

GALLANT, A, *Principles and Techniques for the Beauty Specialist*, Stanley Thorns

GOLDBERG, A G, *Body Massage for the Beauty Therapist*, Heinemann 1972

GREENBLATT, R, *The Hirsute Female*

HINKEL A, *Electrolysis, Thermolysis and the Blend*, Arroway Publishers 1968

KENTON, L, *Ageless Ageing*, Century Arrow 1985

KENTON, L, *Biogenic Diet*, Century Hutchinson 1986

KENTON, L, *The Joy of Beauty*, Century Arrow 1983

MAURY, M, *The Secret of Life and Youth*, Macdonald 1964

MINDELL, E, *The Vitamin Bible*, Arlington Books 1984

MONTAGNA W, *Structure and Function of the Skin*, Academic Press 1974

MOORHOUSE, L, *Total Fitness*, Granada 1976

MORRIS, J D, *Manicure and Pedicure Handbook*, Batsford 1986

MURRAY, D, *Scientific Skin Care*, Arlington Books 1983

OGLE, J, *Age Proofing*, Arlington Books 1984

ORBACH, S, *Fat is a Feminist Issue*, Hamlyn Paperbacks 1978

PREHODA, R W, *Extended Youth*, Peter Owens 1970

RYMAN, D, *Aromatherapy Handbook*, Century 1984

SAMMAN, P D, *The Nails in Disease*, Heinemann 1978

SCOTT, P M, *Clayton's Electrotherapy and Actinotherapy*, Balliere, Tyndall 1975

SCOTT BELLER, A, *Fat and Thin*, Macgraw Hill 1977

SKAWINSKA, V, *A Question of Weight*, Michel Lafon 1982

SOLOMANS, B, *Lecture Notes on Dermatology*, Blackwell Scientific 1973

SPIRA, M, *The No Diet Book*, Fontana Paperbacks 1982

STUART, R, *Act Thin, Stay Thin*, Granada 1978

TAYLOR, E, *Figure Control*, John Murray 1963

TISSERAND, R, *The Art of Aromatherapy*, C W Daniel 1977

WILLIAMS, M, *Therapeutic Exercise*, W B Saunders 1957

WURTMAN, J, *The Carbohydrate Cravers Diet*, Arlington Books 1984

YOUNG, A, *Practical Cosmetic Science*, Mills and Boon 1972

Useful addresses

General

The Association of Suntanning Operators (ASTO)
32 Grayshott Road, London SW11

The British Association of Electrolysists
16 Quakers Mede, Haddenham, Bucks, HP17 8EB

City and Guilds of London Institute
46 Brittania Street, London WC1X 9RG

*The Confederation of International Beauty and Cosmetology and
The British Association of Beauty Therapy and Cosmetology*
The Secretariat, Suite 5, Wolseley House, Oriel Road,
Cheltenham GL50 1TH

Health and Beauty Salon Magazine
Quadrant House, The Quadrant, Sutton, Surrey SM2

The Institute of Electrolysis
251 Seymour Grove, Manchester M16 0DS

*The International Health and Beauty Council and
The International Federation of Health and Beauty Therapists
and The International Institute of Sports Therapy*
109a Felpham Road, Felpham, West Sussex PO22 7PW

ITEC
16 Avenue Place, Harrogate, HG2 7PJ

The Registrar of Business Names
2nd Floor, Companies House, 55–71 City Road, London
EC1Y 2DN

Equipment suppliers

Aston and Fincher
8 Holyhead Road, Handsworth, Birmingham
This cash and carry supplier has showrooms in Bristol,
Coventry, Cardiff, Swansea, Plymouth, Nottingham,
Liverpool, Hull and Worcester

Beauty Equipment Centre
Antonia House, 262 Holloway Road, London N7

Depilex Ltd
Regent House, Dock Road, Birkenhead, Merseyside L41
1DG

Du-Lac Epilation Equipment
Johanna Lack, 1 Albion Villas, The Leas, Folkestone, Kent

Ellisons (Mail order and two showrooms)
7 Hawley Road, Hinckley, Leicestershire

House of Famuir
Beeston Grange, Sandy, Bedfordshire

Laboratoire Dr Renaud
Unit 5, Vaughan Road, Heaton Norris, Stockport, Cheshire

Nordic Saunas
Holland Road, Oxted, Surrey

Original Additions
Cash and carry showrooms, 29 Smith Street, London SW3
4EP

Oritree Ltd
3 Moxon Street, London W1M 3HG

Taylor Reeson Laboratories Ltd
96 Dominion Road, Worthing, Sussex

George Solly Organisation Ltd
James House, Queen Street, Henley on Thames,
Oxfordshire

Beauty books

London Institute of Beauty Culture
247 Tottenham Court Road, London W1P 9AD

Willens Ltd
Howard House, Howard Road, London E11

Nail systems and false nails

Express Nails
601/603 Smithdown Road, Allerton, Liverpool

Fabricius Martin
45 Highlands Heath, Portsmouth Road, London SW15 3TX

Toriess Ltd
Macclesfield Road, Alderley Edge, Cheshire

There are so many good companies supplying cosmetics, treatments creams and all manner of materials for the beauty therapist that it would be impossible to list them all, so the reader is recommended to study the trade press and also attend exhibitions where a wide range of the goods are on display.

Index